CW00586093

LONDON
UNDERGROUND
GUIDE 2015

Written by Jason Cross

Edited by Nick Meskell

Published by Train Crazy Publishing
© 2015 Train Crazy Publishing

Published by:
Train Crazy Publishing, Videoscene, PO Box 243, Lytham St Annes. FY8 9DE
email: sales@videoscene.co.uk

Contents

Introduction

Following on from the 'London Underground Guide 2014', this is the fully revised and re-written second edition, updated to the beginning of 2015. The London Underground is the world's oldest metro system, which has developed over its 152 year history into the system that we see before us today. This book aims to describe each of the eleven lines and the different types of trains used, along with some handy tips on using the system, a guide to engineering trains and a fleet list, all in a pocket sized book that can be a handy companion to any journey on the Underground.

The book is written by an enthusiast, and is aimed mainly at enthusiasts, but can also be a good source of information for visitors to London who might like to know a little more about the fascinating system they are travelling on. With a book of this size it is impossible to describe every aspect of the Underground's operation in great detail, and information such as timetables, opening hours, which stations have step free access etc are not included. This is covered by information provided by Transport for London on their continually updated website at **www.tfl.gov.uk**

The information contained in this book has been obtained from official sources and from our own observations. The author and editor would like to thank many members of TfL staff who have been most helpful, and Brian Hardy for his invaluable advice and assistance. All of the images in the book were taken by the author, and included amongst them are several views from the cab, which were taken with full official permission.

Jason Cross
February 2015

Content - The information provided in this book has been obtained from official sources as well as our observations, updated to 27th February 2015.

Maps - Excluding the official underground map on pages 8/9, the individual line maps used in this publication are our own versions. These are to be used only as a rough guide. Connections to railway stations and other lines are not shown. Not all of the stations are open all of the day or at weekends and some do not have step-free access. Please use the official TfL map provided or check with TfL before travelling.

Front cover: A train of 1995 Stock led by 51538 arrives at Mornington Crescent with a northbound Northern Line service for Edgware on 27 December 2014.

Back cover: A train of 1996 Stock led by driving motor 96100 arrives in the northbound Jubilee Line platform at Baker Street with a service for Stanmore on 13 December 2014.

Welcome to the London Underground

Tube Lines:

- Bakerloo Line
- Central Line
- Jubilee Line
- Northern Line
- Piccadilly Line
- Victoria Line
- Waterloo & City Line

Sub Surface Lines:

- Circle Line
- District Line
- Hammersmith & City Line
- Metropolitan Line

The lines of the London Underground

With 249 route miles and 270 stations, the London Underground is one of the most complex metro systems in the world. It carries an average of four million passengers per day, which is more than the rest of the UK railway network (which carries approximately 2.75 million passengers per day). At the time of writing, the record stood at 4.56 million passengers carried on 14 November 2014. It is also the oldest underground railway in the world, and the section between Paddington and Farringdon dates back to 1863.

The network is divided up into 11 different lines, each of which have their own name and colour for ease of identification on maps and signs. Commonly known as 'the tube', only seven of the 11 lines are actually tube lines, the other four being what are known as 'sub surface' lines. The difference between the two is quite obvious when a train of Tube Stock is seen alongside a train of Surface Stock as the tube trains are much smaller. The sub surface lines were built using the 'cut and cover' method, where a trench was dug in the road, tracks laid in the bottom of the trench and then the road rebuilt over the top. This was a very disruptive method of construction, and later lines were built in tube tunnels at a much deeper level and were bored through the ground without disturbing life on the surface. The tunnels of the tube lines were of a smaller diameter than those on the sub surface lines, so the trains which operate on the tube lines are much smaller than those on the sub surface lines, the latter being approximately the same size as trains which operate on Network Rail. Despite the fact that four lines of the system are not tube lines, Transport for London refer publicly to the whole system as the 'tube', and it has become an almost affectionate nickname for the system.

Of the 249 route miles, only 113 miles of the system are in tunnel (20 miles of sub surface and 93 miles of tube), which means that only 45% of the London Underground is actually under the ground, with the remainder being above ground and out in the open.

The difference between Surface Stock and Tube Stock is very apparent in this photograph of a train of Jubilee Line 1996 Stock being overtaken by a Metropolitan Line train of S Stock at Kilburn. 10 September 2014.

Changes Since the 2014 Guide Book

Since the release of the London Underground Guide 2014, the introduction of new S Stock trains has continued with the new trains now working all services on the Metropolitan Line, the Hammersmith & City Line and Circle Line, and some services on the District Line. Their introduction to the District saw the withdrawal of the last of the C Stock trains with the last of the type operating in passenger service on 3 June 2014, with a final railtour running over former C Stock routes on 29 June. Driving Motor 5721 has been saved by the London Transport Museum, 5720 has been donated to a school in Plumstead and 5701 is a static classroom at the Royal Greenwich University Technical College, all other vehicles having been despatched from London by road for scrap. Next to be replaced by the S Stock is the D Stock, and the first trains of this type were withdrawn on 19 January 2015. The D Stock will be the final type of train to be replaced by the S Stock.

The introduction of the TBTC 'moving block' signalling on the Northern Line was completed and the final section of line to be converted to automatic operation between Belsize Park and Edgware went live on 1 June 2014.

A change to the way people pay for their travel was introduced on 16 September 2014 when contactless payment using a debit card was introduced on the Underground having previously been introduced on London buses.

The battery loco fleet continues to be given life extension modifications, although there are still quite a few un-rebuilt examples in service. The Schöma diesel locomotive fleet is undergoing a more drastic change with their diesel power units being swapped for batteries. The first two pairs of locomotives were being converted at Clayton's in Burton-on-Trent at the time of writing.

A 24 hour Underground service on Friday and Saturday nights is set to be introduced from 12 September 2015. This will apply to parts of the Piccadilly, Northern and Central lines and the entire lengths of both the Jubilee and Victoria lines.

Planning and consultation are underway to extend the south end of the Bakerloo Line towards Hayes, while approval has been given to build a new branch of the Northern Line to Battersea. A design concept for a 'New Tube for London' has also been unveiled, and it is proposed that this train will replace the current fleet on the Central, Waterloo & City, Bakerloo and Piccadilly lines. These extensions and new trains are all plans for the future which will not come to fruition during 2015, and will no doubt be subject to change in the meantime, so are not covered elsewhere in this book.

End of an era:
After serving the capital since 1970, 2014 saw the C Stock bow out of service at the hands of new trains of S Stock. A final railtour was run on 29 June 2014, and is seen here with 5578 on the rear passing through Baker Street on the final leg of the tour to Hammersmith.

Ticketing

The London Underground (and other London transport modes) is split into zones. Zone 1 is the central area, with zone 6 being the outer section. There are also zones 7 to 9 which cover the Metropolitan Line north of Moor Park to Watford, Amersham and Chesham. The zones used and the number of zones passed through during a journey determine the price, with zone 1 being the most expensive. The zones are displayed on the Underground map.

The most popular way of paying for travel in London is with an Oyster card. This is a credit card sized plastic card onto which users can pre-load season tickets or add credit with which travel can be paid for on a 'pay as you go' basis. They can be used on all Underground trains, National Rail trains in the London area, London Buses, Docklands Light Railway and Tramlink.

When used as a 'pay as you go' card, the user 'touches in' at the start of their journey on a yellow pad on the ticket gate, and then 'touches out' on the ticket gate at the end of their journey. It may also sometimes be necessary to touch again at an interchange point. The Oyster system then calculates the cheapest fare for the journey made and deducts it from the credit on the card. If multiple journeys are made during a day, the Oyster system will stop charging the user once the daily price cap is reached. The Oyster system is time based, and it expects users to 'touch out' within a certain time after 'touching in'. It isn't really designed to be used by people who may wish to break their journey to watch trains go by. If you go over the time limits, the system can be fooled into charging extra for journeys that it thinks you have made in that time. If using Oyster to watch trains, then it is recommended that you keep a close eye on how long it has been since you last touched, and it is recommended that you view the relevant page on the TFL website which gives details of all the time limits applicable across the various zones. This can be found at:

http://www.tfl.gov.uk/fares-and-payments/oyster/using-oyster/maximum-journey-times

The 'Contactless' method of payment was introduced in September 2014. This allows the user to pay for journeys with their contactless debit card. It operates in the same way as 'pay as you go' on Oyster, except that there is no need to add money to the card at any point as the system takes the money direct from the user's bank account, thus eradicating the need to use a ticket machine, ticket office or the TFL website to add credit. There is of course one big downside to this, which is that if you have an Oyster card in your wallet close to a contactless card, and you touch your wallet on the card reader, the system may well charge the card you did not intend to use. Regular announcements are made across the Underground system warning of what is described as 'card clash'.

The ticket gates at Sudbury Town station. The yellow Oyster pads can be seen on top of the upright, and the slot for scanning paper tickets is situated in the front of the upright. Touching a valid Oyster card or passing a valid ticket will open the paddle gates to allow the passage of one person. Sudbury Town station is a listed building as it is an early example of one of designer Charles Holden's 'brick box with concrete lid' stations.

ets are still available and can be purchased from machines or ticket offices
ork. The best to use for railway enthusiasts is the One Day Travelcard wh
s either a zone 1-6 or a zone 1-9. Unless you are travelling north of Moor
tan, a zone 1-6 covers everything. There are no time limits with these, an
siast the chance to pause to watch trains without having to worry about
to 'touch out'. The price of these tickets rose at the start of 2015 to encou
ntactless or Oyster, and there is now a gap between the daily price cap on
of a paper One Day Travelcard when used in the peak. The Oyster and
e cap across zones 1 to 6 is £11.70 which applies to both peak and off pea
one 1 to 6 Travelcard is £17.00 if purchased before 9.30am, and £12 if purc

or of this book recommends the use of a paper One Day Travelcard if you a
ugh journeys to make it worthwhile and intend to break your journey fr
ns. If you are only going to make a small number of journeys and can touc
time limits, or you do not intend to pause to watch trains, then Oyster or
way to pay for your travel.

n London is quite complex as it has to meet a whole host of needs across a
rt, so the above overview and advice is certainly not the complete pictur
methods are subject to change and the above information should only b
de. For further information, it is recommended that a visit is made to the
w.tfl.gov.uk under the heading 'Fares and Payments'.

ces at Underground stations are expected to be phased out during 2015.

nside the ticket hall at Maida Vale on the Bakerloo Line, showing the tw
Underground mosaics which have been resto ed

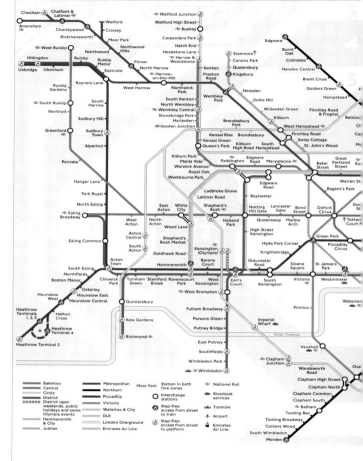

Legend

Bakerloo	Metropolitan	Moor Park ● Station in both fare zones
Central	Northern	◯ Interchange stations
Circle	Piccadilly	◉ Step-free access from street to train
District open weekends, public holidays and some Olympia events	Victoria	Ⓐ Step-free access from street to platform
Hammersmith & City	Waterloo & City	National Rail
Jubilee	London Overground	Riverboat services
	Emirates Air Line	Tramlink
		✈ Airport
		Emirates Air Line

MAYOR OF LONDON

 tfl.gov.uk

 24 hour travel information
0343 222 1234*

*Service and network charges may apply. See tfl.gov.uk/terms for details.

Improvement works may affect y

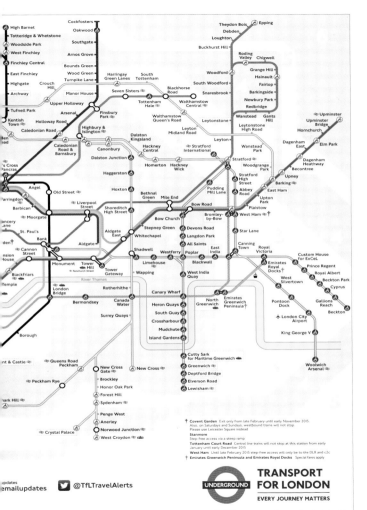

† **Covent Garden** Exit only from late February until early November 2015
Also, on Saturdays and Sundays, westbound trains will not stop.
Please use Leicester Square instead

Stanmore
Step-free access via a steep ramp

Tottenham Court Road Central line trains will not stop at this station from early
January until early December 2015

West Ham Until late February 2015 step-free access will only be to the DLR and c2c

† **Emirates Greenwich Peninsula and Emirates Royal Docks** Special fares apply

updates
emailupdates

🐦 @TfLTravelAlerts

UNDERGROUND

TRANSPORT FOR LONDON

EVERY JOURNEY MATTERS

se check before you travel

Version J TfL 12.2014

Correct at time of going to print

BAKERLOO LINE →

OVERVIEW

Route: Elephant & Castle to Harrow & Wealdstone
Type of route / operation: Tube / manually driven with conventional signalling
First section opened: Baker Street to Kennington Road (now Lambeth North) opened by the Baker Street & Waterloo Railway on 10 March 1906
Route mileage: 14.4 miles
Number of stations: 25
Trains: 1972 MkII Tube Stock, with a few cars converted from 1972 MkI Tube Stock (max of 32 trains required at peak times)
Depot(s): Stonebridge Park
Stabling points: Queen's Park / Elephant & Castle / London Road

HISTORY

The Bakerloo began life as the Baker Street & Waterloo Railway, the first section of which opened between Baker Street and Kennington Road on 10 March 1906. On 5 August of the same year, the line opened beyond Kennington Road to the current terminus at Elephant & Castle. The first extension north of Baker Street opened to Great Central (now called Marylebone) on 27 March 1907, and then to Edgware Road on 15 June 1907. The line was further extended to Paddington with backing from the Great Western Railway, and this section opened on 1 December 1913. The next section from Paddington to Queen's Park was opened in stages during 1915, and once Queen's Park was reached, the Bakerloo was able to join the London & North Western Railway's London Euston to Watford Junction Line (often referred to as the Watford DC Line) with Bakerloo trains running through to Willesden Junction initially and then through to Watford Junction from 16 April 1917.

With the Metropolitan Railway's branches from Stanmore, Watford, Uxbridge, Chesham and Amersham and beyond all feeding into the two track tunnel section between Finchley Road and Baker Street, this section became very congested. To ease this, as part of the 1935-40 New Works Programme, new tube tunnels were built between Baker Street and Finchley Road. These new tunnels, and the Metropolitan's Stanmore branch, became part of the Bakerloo with the Stanmore branch being taken over by the Bakerloo on 20 November 1939. Baker Street thus became a junction on the Bakerloo. With southbound trains from Watford Junction and Stanmore having their own platforms, but northbound trains having to share one platform regardless of which branch they were serving, it wasn't long before Baker Street became congested. To ease this, a fourth platform was built at Baker Street to serve a new line beyond Baker Street to Charing Cross. This became the Jubilee Line which took over the Stanmore branch from the Bakerloo from 1 May 1979. The junction still exists today and acts as a link between the Jubilee and the Bakerloo and is mainly used to allow engineer's trains to and from Ruislip depot to reach the Bakerloo. This left the Bakerloo with just the Elephant & Castle to Watford Junction line, but services to Watford Junction were reduced and then withdrawn altogether in 1982, trains terminating instead at Stonebridge Park. From 1984, services were re-introduced north of Stonebridge Park, but only as far as Harrow & Wealdstone, the current northern terminus of the Bakerloo.

Stonebridge Park station with a Harrow & Wealdstone bound train led by 3554 arriving under a moonlit dusk sky. The silver hut to the right of the train is used by station staff who check that all passengers have alighted from trains that terminate here and go into Stonebridge Park depot to reverse. 10 August 2014.

THE ROUTE

Harrow & Wealdstone

The northern terminus of the Bakerloo is at Harrow & Wealdstone. Trains arriving from the south arrive in platform 1 and detrain before proceeding into a central reversing siding. The line continues beyond here to Watford Junction, and this section is served by London Overground services to and from London Euston, and which share tracks with the Bakerloo between Harrow & Wealdstone and Queen's Park. After the driver has changed ends, the empty Bakerloo train will exit the reversing siding and enter platform 2. Platforms 3 to 6 are on the tracks of the West Coast Main Line and are served by various slow and semi fast services. Interchange between the Bakerloo and WCML services is possible by means of a footbridge. Harrow & Wealdstone is remembered for the terrible crash on the morning of 8 October 1952, when a Perth to Euston express crashed into the rear of a local train which was stopped in the platform, and then moments later the wreckage was run into by a Euston to Liverpool and Manchester express. The death toll reached 112, and a memorial plaque is located on the station building.

Kenton

The first station is Kenton which was opened by the LNWR in June 1912 and served by Bakerloo trains from 16 April 1917. The station retains LNWR platform buildings and canopies. There are no platforms here to serve the adjacent WCML, there have only ever been platforms on the Bakerloo / Watford DC tracks.

The line now passes beneath the Metropolitan Main Line and Network Rail's Aylesbury lines which pass overhead on a large bridge which spans the Bakerloo / London Overground and WCML tracks.

South Kenton

This station consists of a single island platform serving only the Bakerloo and London Overground. Access to the station is from a subway which also serves as a pedestrian tunnel under the railway linking residential areas on either side of the line. The station was built in 1933 and is to a concrete and glass 'art deco' design. Due to a lack of space, there are no ticket barriers installed at this station.

North Wembley

Another station built by the LNWR to serve only the tracks of the Watford DC tracks and very similar in design to the station two stops further north at Kenton.

Wembley Central

The next stop at Wembley Central first had a station on this site in 1842 when Sudbury & Wembley was opened by the London & Birmingham Railway. Today's station bears no resemblance to that though and is quite a modern structure with several buildings constructed over the top of it. When the Bakerloo first reached here on 16 April 1917, the station was called Wembley for Sudbury, the current Wembley Central name not being applied until July 1948. There are platform faces on the WCML here and these are served by a small number of London Midland and Southern services and interchange is possible between these and the Bakerloo and London Overground.

Heading south from Wembley Central, the Bakerloo / London Overground tracks dive down and pass beneath the WCML and the north end of the Wembley freight yard complex to emerge on the opposite side of the WCML alongside the Bakerloo's Stonebridge Park depot.

Stonebridge Park

Stonebridge Park station is quite modern at platform level, but the original station building still survives down at street level. Some Bakerloo trains from central London terminate here, and then proceed into the depot throat to reverse. At a higher level alongside the station are Stonebridge Park carriage sidings, and quite often the Scotrail sleeping trains can be seen here being serviced. Immediately south of the station, the Bakerloo crosses over the top of the A406 North Circular Road.

Harlesden

Harlesden retains much of its LNWR appearance both at platform level and also with the station building at street level.

Willesden Junction

This is a large island platform with a central bay, however the central bay can only be used by London Overground trains, Bakerloo trains being too long to fit. Connection is available here with further Overground services which call at the high level station on the North London Line above and also with several bus routes which call at the station. Alongside the station is a connection between the Wembley freight yards and the North London Line which sees a regular flow of freight traffic.

As Bakerloo trains head south from Willesden Junction, they pass the London Overground Willesden depot before curving to come alongside the West Coast Main Line tracks once more.

Kensal Green

This station is situated at the London end of the 317 yard long Kensal Green tunnel. Opened on 1 October 1916, the platform buildings are of LNWR construction. The station entrance building is at street level above and was built alongside the original and opened in 1980, after which the original building was demolished.

A northbound train led by 3545 arrives at Kensal Green on 10 August 2014. It will be noted that the Tube Stock is lower than the platform edge. The platforms at stations between Kensal Green and Harrow & Wealdstone are at a compromise height so that the step down to Tube Stock is roughly the same as the step up to London Overground stock, making it difficult to apply step free access on this section of railway.

Queen's Park

At the country end of Queen's Park North Shed the southbound Bakerloo Line splits away from the southbound Watford DC Line, and the northbound Bakerloo Line joins the northbound Watford DC Line. The North Shed performs multiple roles. By night, it is a carriage shed used for stabling trains during non-traffic hours. By day, roads 21 and 24 form the northbound and southbound Bakerloo lines with trains in passenger service actually passing through the shed. Roads 22 and 23 are used for reversing trains which have terminated at Queen's Park. The station consists of four platforms under a fine overall roof. The inner platforms 2 and 3 are served by the Bakerloo, with the outer platforms 1 and 4 served by London Overground services to and from Euston. There are also two platforms numbered 5 and 6 that serve the slow lines of the WCML, however, no trains are currently booked to call at these. South of the station is the south carriage shed (roads 25 and 26) which is used to stable up to four trains. The up and down tracks of the Watford DC Line are on either side of the Bakerloo's formation, with the Bakerloo's tracks descending as they pass alongside the south carriage shed to enter the tube tunnels which will take them all the way to Elephant & Castle. It is also possible for Bakerloo Line trains to continue towards Euston on the Watford DC Line and the centre conductor rail is in place as far as the next station at Kilburn High Road. This is to allow Bakerloo trains arriving at Queen's Park from the north to reverse using the crossover at Kilburn High Road. It is rare to see this move in daylight, but there is an as required timetabled move at the end of traffic hours which is used to keep the centre rail rust free. The best chance of seeing a Bakerloo train at Kilburn High Road during daylight is if the tunnels south of Queen's Park are closed, but the section north of Queen's Park still has a Bakerloo service operating.

13

Kilburn Park

This station boasts a fine grade II listed station building finished in dark red tiles to a design by Stanley Heaps. Of note is a glass dome situated above the escalators. When opened on 31 January 1915, this station formed the temporary terminus of the Bakerloo for a few days until the section to Queen's Park was opened on 11 February.

Maida Vale

Another station with a Stanley Heaps designed red tiled station building, which is also grade II listed. Inside the main entrance are two London Underground mosaics which have been superbly restored (see page 7). This station was not ready when the line was extended through to Kilburn Park and Queen's Park, with trains non-stopping until 6 June 1915.

Warwick Avenue

This station serves the 'Little Venice' area and is close to where the Regent's Canal meets the Grand Union Canal. It is a simple two platform tube station with a sub surface ticket hall and no station buildings at street level.

Paddington

Here the Bakerloo Line interchanges not only with the Paddington mainline terminus, but also with the Hammersmith & City, Circle and District lines. The sharply curved platforms here are decorated with a design celebrating the tunnel boring machine and the Greathead shield. To the north of the platforms there is a crossover which sees use to turn back trains only at times of service disruption.

Inside the Leslie Green designed station building at Edgware Road showing the ticket office area and gateline. 10 January 2015.

Edgware Road

Although the station on the Bakerloo is close to the Edgware Road station serving the Hammersmith & City, District and Circle lines, there is no direct link between the two stations and it is not listed as an interchange on any tube maps. Opened in June 1907 as a terminus, the station became a through station with the opening of the Paddington extension in 1913. It retains its original red tiled street level building designed by Leslie Green.

Marylebone

Marylebone opened in March 1907 as Great Central after the name of the railway company that served the Marylebone mainline terminus above. It was renamed Marylebone on 15 April 1917. At the north end of the northbound platform, the name Great Central can still be seen in the tiles on the wall.

Baker Street

The Bakerloo platforms at Baker Street are decorated with silhouettes of the fictional character Sherlock Holmes who supposedly lived at 221b Baker Street. If you look closely at these silhouettes, it will be noted that they are made up of lots of tiny Sherlock silhouettes. There is cross platform interchange here with the Jubilee Line. The Baker Street to Stanmore section of the Jubilee used to be a part of the Bakerloo, and a connection still exists between the two lines, used now by engineering trains gaining access to and from the Bakerloo Line.

Regent's Park

This is one of the quietest stations in Central London with roughly 3 million passengers per year starting or finishing their journeys here (compared to 70 million at the next station Oxford Circus). The station has no surface buildings and is accessed by a subway on the Marylebone Road.

Oxford Circus

Oxford Circus serves the busy west end shopping area. The station also forms an interchange between the Bakerloo, the Central and the Victoria lines.

Piccadilly Circus

Interchange between the Bakerloo and the Piccadilly is available here. The Bakerloo platforms are quite unusual in that a trailing crossover at the north end of the slightly staggered platforms occupies part of the station tunnel, and there is an open section where both the southbound and northbound tracks share the same tunnel. The crossover is only used at times of service disruption. Only the 1972 Stock is allowed to traverse this crossover due to limited clearances. Battery locos engaged on engineering duties, being longer than the 1972 Stock vehicles, are prohibited from crossing over here. Tight curves at the north end of the platforms leave a rather large gap between the platform edge and the trains and passengers are reminded via announcements and signage to 'mind the gap'.

Charing Cross

Originally named Trafalgar Square, the station was renamed to Charing Cross in 1979 when it became part of a station complex which included the Northern Line's Strand station and the new Jubilee Line terminus. The station has entrances in Trafalgar Square, The Strand and in Charing Cross mainline station. Interchange is possible here with the Northern Line, but the Jubilee Line station is now closed following the opening of the Jubilee Line extension.

Embankment

Situated at the country end of Charing Cross mainline station, Embankment station is served by the Bakerloo and the Northern at deep level, and also by the Circle and District at sub-surface level. For much of 2014, the deep level platforms were closed for replacement of the escalators with Northern and Bakerloo trains non-stopping. These platforms re-opened in November 2014 and the station once again provides interchange between all lines. Opened as Embankment, the station was renamed Charing Cross (Embankment) in 1914, renamed again to just Charing Cross in 1915, and then it regained the name Charing Cross (Embankment) in 1974. Finally, the station was renamed to Embankment in 1976. South of this station, the Bakerloo tunnels pass beneath the River Thames, and at some points are only a few feet below the river bed. With the fear that German bombing may penetrate the tunnels during World War II, floodgates were installed at the platform ends at Embankment and also at Waterloo in 1939.

During traffic hours, London Road sidings are usually nearly empty, but outside of traffic hours they are used to stable ten trains. On 10 August 2014, just one train of 1972 MkII Stock was present with DM 3546 at the north end. The train behind it is of 1967 Stock that is used for training cleaners.

Waterloo
One of the busiest interchanges on the Underground, the Bakerloo meets the Northern (Charing Cross branch), Jubilee and Waterloo & City lines, as well as the mainline station above ground.

Lambeth North
Lambeth North was the first southern terminus of the Bakerloo as it opened on 10 March 1906 as Kennington Road. It was renamed to Westminster Bridge Road in July of that year, before finally taking its current name in April 1917. The station ceased to be a terminus when the section of line to Elephant & Castle opened on 5 August 1906.

Just to the north of Lambeth North station, there is a scissors crossover and a junction with a short branch turning off to the west. This goes to London Road depot where a number of trains are stabled when not in service. When entering service, some trains leave London Road depot, and then start a northbound journey from Waterloo, while others reverse and run empty to Elephant & Castle and enter service from there. At the end of service, the same happens in reverse. Only when a train is going into London Road depot during traffic hours, is anything other than Elephant & Castle displayed as the destination on a southbound train south of

Queen's Park, as they display Waterloo instead. London Road depot is in the open and can be viewed from the corner of St George's Road and Lambeth Road in London SE1, close to the Imperial War Museum. It is usually nearly empty during the day, but ten Bakerloo trains stable here at night. There are also four cars of 1967 Stock that are used for training purposes which reside here.

Elephant & Castle

As trains approach Elephant & Castle, they are greeted by a scissors crossover. This allows trains to arrive and depart from either platform of this two platform terminus. To the south of the station platforms the tunnels continue for a short distance and there is room to stable up to two trains. Interchange is available between the Bakerloo and the Northern below ground, and also with the Network Rail station above ground.

OPERATIONS

The 1972 Stock is not equipped to work automatically, so the Bakerloo is a manually driven line with conventional signalling. From Queen's Park southwards, the signalling is controlled by London Underground, but north of Queen's Park, the signalling is controlled by Network Rail and is of the 3 aspect red, yellow, green type, but with LU train stop protection (the class 378 London Overground units are fitted with tripcocks).

Under normal operating conditions, except for at the start and end of traffic hours, all southbound trains run through to the southern terminus at Elephant & Castle. In the northbound direction, roughly two thirds of trains reverse at Queen's Park, with the rest running through to either Stonebridge Park or Harrow & Wealdstone. At the end of traffic hours, some southbound trains terminate at Waterloo and then run empty into London Road sidings for stabling, with the reverse happening at the start of traffic.

First Trains:

Northbound (Mon-Sat):	0515 Stonebridge Park to Harrow & Wealdstone
Southbound (Mon-Sat):	0526 Stonebridge Park to Elephant & Castle
Northbound (Sun):	0700 Stonebridge to Harrow & Wealdstone
Southbound (Sun):	0714 Queen's Park to Elephant & Castle

Last Trains:

Northbound (Mon-Sat):	0023 Elephant & Castle to Queen's Park (0050)
Southbound (Mon-Sat):	0031 Harrow & Wealdstone to Queen's Park (0053)
Northbound (Sun):	2337 Elephant & Castle to Harrow & Wealdstone (0026)
Southbound (Sun):	0013 Harrow & Wealdstone to Queen's Park (0035)

JUBILEE LINE →

OVERVIEW

Route: Stanmore to Stratford
Type of route / operation: Tube / automatic
First section opened: Stanmore to Wembley Park by the Metropolitan Railway on
10 December 1932
Route mileage: 22.5 miles
Number of stations: 27
Trains: 1996 Tube Stock (max of 58 trains required at peak times)
Depot(s): Stratford Market
Stabling points: Stanmore / Neasden

HISTORY

The Jubilee did not open until 1979, but parts of the line have a history which goes back before that. The northern terminus at Stanmore was opened by the Metropolitan as a branch from Wembley Park on 10 December 1932. With Metropolitan trains converging on the two track tunnel section south of Finchley Road to Baker Street from Uxbridge, Watford, Chesham, Aylesbury and beyond and now Stanmore, this tunnel section quickly became congested. As part of the 'New Works Programme' of 1935-40, a new section of tube tunnel was built from the Bakerloo at Baker Street to Finchley Road. This new tunnel section became part of the Bakerloo, which also took over the Stanmore branch from the Metropolitan on 20 November 1939. At Baker Street, southbound Bakerloo trains from the Watford Junction branch and from the Stanmore branch both ran into separate platforms, but northbound trains heading for either branch had to share the same platform. This later became another cause of congestion and led to the building of a new platform at Baker Street at the same time as a new tunnel section was built from Baker Street to Charing Cross. From 1 May 1979, the Stanmore branch became the Jubilee Line with services operating between Stanmore and Charing Cross, totally separate to the Bakerloo which was now reduced to Elephant & Castle to Watford Junction. Further extension came in the 1990s with the Jubilee Line Extension (JLE) which took the line through Westminster, Waterloo, Southwark and Bermondsey into Docklands and on to a new terminus at Stratford. This line opened in stages during 1999 with through services over the whole route commencing on 20 November of that year. The JLE turns away from the original line just south of Green Park, meaning that the terminus at Charing Cross was not incorporated and is now disused, although trains can run to there out of service to reverse at times of disruption. Charing Cross is also sometimes used for filming and to stable engineering trains.

The JLE was opened as a conventionally signalled railway, but the whole of the Jubilee is now operated automatically using the Transmission Based Train Control (TBTC) moving block system. Automatic operation was introduced between Dollis Hill and Stratford / Charing Cross on 29 December 2010 (stage one) and between Dollis Hill and Stanmore on 26 June 2011 (stage two).

Perhaps confusing to some, trains are described as northbound and southbound between Stanmore and Green Park, but on the JLE, trains are referred to as eastbound and westbound.

The terminus at Stanmore on 4 October 2014, with 96124 in platform 1 and 96028 in platform 3. A third train can be seen in the background in platform 2.

THE ROUTE

Stanmore

The northern terminus of the Jubilee is at Stanmore in Middlesex. The station and line was opened by the Metropolitan Railway in 1932 and the Metropolitan station building still exists and forms the main entrance from street level, although the ticket office has been moved down to platform level to where a newer entrance from the car park now enters the station. Between the station and the car park there is a fan of sidings where trains stable outside traffic hours. The addition of a third platform at Stanmore has caused a little confusion as the other two platforms were not renumbered to match and east to west, the platforms in order are platform 2, platform 1 and then the new platform 3.

Canons Park

Originally called Canons Park (Edgware), the suffix was dropped after just one year. The station is on an embankment and is accessed by stairs from street level.

Queensbury

This station was opened in December 1934 in what were more or less open fields at the time. The idea was that the new station would encourage residential development in the area which would then generate additional revenue for the Metropolitan Railway. A name was needed for this new station, and with the next station called Kingsbury, it was decided to call this station Queensbury. Of interest here are the station buildings and large roundabout on which is mounted a large roundel.

Kingsbury

Opened with the line on 10 December 1932, Kingsbury is the final stop on the Stanmore branch before Wembley Park. The station building is on a bridge over the tracks here, and the height between rail level and the underside of the bridge still gives away the fact that this line was built for full height stock.

South of Kingsbury, the line passes alongside the Fryent Country Park before passing beneath the southbound tracks of the Metropolitan Line on the approach to Wembley Park.

Wembley Park

At Wembley Park, the Jubilee occupies the centre two platforms in the station with the northbound and southbound Metropolitan lines on either side. If travelling into central London it is often quicker to change onto the Metropolitan Line here as the Met runs non-stop between here and Finchley Road, whereas the Jubilee makes five station stops.

At the north end of the station there is a centre reversing siding which is used to turn back trains from the south. Heading south from Wembley Park, the Jubilee has a physical connection with the Metropolitan as part of the complex of tracks which form the north entrance/exit to/from Neasden depot. The two tracks of the National Rail Chiltern Line are also alongside and will remain parallel with the Jubilee and Metropolitan as far as Finchley Road. The Jubilee now passes right alongside Neasden depot, and although this is considered to be a Metropolitan Line depot, several Jubilee Line trains also stable here.

Neasden

The station was opened by the Metropolitan Railway as Kingsbury and Neasden on 2 August 1880. The name was changed to Neasden and Kingsbury in 1910, but with the opening of Kingsbury station on the Stanmore branch in 1932, the name was changed to just Neasden. Metropolitan trains ceased to call here after 1940, although the station still has platforms on the Met lines which can be used at times of disruption.

Dollis Hill

Opened in 1909 by the Metropolitan Railway, this station consists of an island platform with platform faces only on the Jubilee. Access to the station platform is via subways.

Willesden Green

Opened by the Metropolitan Railway in November 1879, in a similar fashion to Neasden, this station still has platforms on the Met lines which can be used at times of disruption. Of interest here is the station building at street level which dates from 1925 and still bears the words 'Metropolitan Railway'. A centre reversing siding is situated between the Jubilee tracks north of the platforms for turning back trains from the south.

Kilburn

Another island platform with faces only on the Jubilee. Access from street level below is via stairs or lift. Immediately south of the station is an impressive steel bridge over the Kilburn High Road which bears the name of the Metropolitan Railway. This can be viewed from street level or from northbound Jubilee or Metropolitan trains.

West Hampstead

After crossing over the top of the North London Line, West Hampstead is reached with yet another central turn back siding for turning back trains from the south situated to the north of the station. The station itself is another island platform, with no platform faces on the Metropolitan. The station was opened by the Metropolitan Railway in June 1879.

Finchley Road

A four platform station on a curve, this station is served by Jubilee and Metropolitan trains and interchange between the two lines is possible here. Heading south, the two lines separate here with the Metropolitan taking the two track tunnel section towards Baker Street while the Jubilee dives down into tube tunnel for the run to Baker Street.

96100 leads a Stanmore bound train into Baker Street on 13 December 2014. This platform was built when the Jubilee Line to Charing Cross was built and opened in 1979. The southbound platform here was the former Bakerloo Line Stanmore branch platform.

Swiss Cottage

Opened as part of the new Bakerloo branch in 1939, Swiss Cottage is a typical 1930s tube station with art-deco uplighters on the escalators, and roundels cast into the ceramic tiles on the platform walls. The opening of this station and the next station at St John's Wood caused the closure of Swiss Cottage, Marlborough Road and Lords stations on the Metropolitan. The Met has run non-stop between Finchley Road and Baker Street ever since.

St John's Wood

Opened at the same time as Swiss Cottage when the new Bakerloo tube line was opened in 1939, this station is very similar at platform level to Swiss Cottage.

Baker Street

This is a very busy interchange, and it is possible to change from the Jubilee onto the Bakerloo, Metropolitan, Hammersmith & City and Circle lines. The northbound platform was newly constructed at the same time as the Charing Cross branch, whereas the southbound platform is the former Bakerloo Stanmore branch southbound platform, although its appearance matches the style of the 1970 built northbound platform. The junction between the Jubilee and Bakerloo still exists in the tunnels either side of the station and is used occasionally by engineering trains to and from Ruislip depot which gain access to the Bakerloo via the Jubilee. Beyond Baker Street in the southbound direction, the tunnels date from the 1970s.

Bond Street

As well as serving the very busy west end shopping area, this station also offers interchange with the Central Line (and in the future, with Crossrail).

It is very difficult to view trains or take photographs of them on the underground section of the Jubilee Line Extension due to the presence of platform edge doors (PEDs). The doors of the train line up with the doors on the platform and both open simultaneously to allow passengers to board and alight. This view was taken from the cab of a train arriving at Southwark and shows the PEDs to great effect.

Green Park

Interchange with the Victoria and Piccadilly Line is available at this station which is situated on Piccadilly adjacent to Green Park and very close to Buckingham Palace. Visible from the south end of the platforms are the junctions where the disused Charing Cross branch continues straight on, and the JLE diverges.

Westminster

This station gives interchange with the District and Circle lines at sub surface level. Here the Jubilee tunnels pass almost beneath the clock tower of the Houses of Parliament and careful monitoring of the position of the tower was required during construction. This station is fitted with Platform Edge Doors (PEDs). Despite what many people believe, the main role of the PEDs is to help manage air flow and not to prevent suicides or people falling off the platforms, although they do perform the latter role very well.

Waterloo

A very busy interchange, it is possible to connect with the Waterloo & City, Northern (Charing Cross branch), Bakerloo and the Waterloo mainline terminus. A rather long moving walkway connects the Jubilee Line with the other Underground lines. PEDs fitted.

Southwark

A fairly quiet station, Southwark offers an interchange with the nearby Waterloo East station. PEDs fitted.

London Bridge

Interchange with the Bank branch of the Northern and with the mainline station above ground is possible here. PEDs fitted.

Bermondsey

Another fairly quiet station with no interchange with other lines. This station is situated on Jamaica Road and is used by just under nine million passengers per year. PEDs fitted.

Canada Water

This station connects with the former East London Line, which is now part of the London Overground network. The stations on the JLE are shining examples of modern design and the circular main entrance is of particular interest. PEDs fitted.

Canary Wharf

Serving the busy Canary Wharf development, this station has become amongst the busiest on the Underground. The station design is one of enormous proportions with lots of open space and circulating areas. Not only does this give the station an airy feel, but it also makes it future proof against increasing passenger numbers. Operationally, this station has a scissors crossover at the west end, allowing trains to be reversed here, although this tends to only happen at times of disruption. PEDs fitted.

North Greenwich

This station has three platforms, 3 is eastbound, 1 is westbound and 2 can be accessed from either end and can be used to reverse trains from either direction. In practice though, it is only used to reverse trains from the west except at times of disruption, and several trains are booked to reverse here. Although there is no interchange with other lines here, this can be a very busy station, especially when there is an event taking place at the nearby O2 Arena (Millennium Dome). There is a large bus interchange here and also the Emirates Air Line, a cable car which crosses the River Thames and offers great views of the dome, Canary Wharf and Docklands area. This station has PEDs fitted.

Heading east, the JLE has already passed beneath the River Thames three times (between Westminster and Waterloo, Canada Water and Canary Wharf and between Canary Wharf and North Greenwich). Leaving North Greenwich towards Stratford, the line passes beneath the Thames for one final time and emerges into daylight on the approach to Canning Town.

Canning Town

This station is a busy interchange with the Docklands Light Railway and also with the adjacent bus station. Being out in the open, this station and the next two at West Ham and Stratford are not fitted with PEDs. The JLE now runs alongside the DLR's Stratford International branch as far as Stratford. The DLR has stations at Star Lane, Abbey Road and Stratford High Street at which the Jubilee does not call.

West Ham

The Jubilee passes beneath the National Rail line into and out of Fenchurch Street and the Hammersmith & City and District lines almost at right angles at West Ham, and there is full interchange between all four lines and also with the DLR.

Stratford

After passing the Jubilee's large Stratford Market Depot and passing beneath Stratford High Street, the terminus of the Jubilee at Stratford is reached. This has three platforms which are almost at right angles to the Central Line and National Rail platforms. There is full interchange here with two lines of the DLR, National Rail, London Overground and the Central Line. There is a large bus interchange alongside the DLR Stratford International branch platforms. The station also serves the busy Westfield shopping centre and the Olympic Park.

Taken from the cab of a train arriving in platform 3 at North Greenwich, a terminating train can be seen in platform 2 with DM 96020 nearest the camera. The platform edge doors can be clearly seen in this picture.

OPERATIONS

Since 26 June 2011, the Jubilee Line has been operated automatically throughout using the Transmission Based Train Control (TBTC) moving block system. The only signals on the line are at Baker Street southbound (controlling access to the Bakerloo) and at Neasden where Jubilee Line trains cross the Metropolitan to access Neasden depot. There are also some fixed train stops at Neasden that would prevent a wrongly signalled Metropolitan Line train from proceeding along the Jubilee. There are no other signals or train stops on the rest of the route, although some of the old signals are still in place but covered over. Trains can be driven manually in 'Protected Manual' mode with speed instructions given to the driver via a screen inside the cab. Trains are driven manually in and out of depots and stabling sidings.

Most trains operate over the full route between Stanmore and Stratford, with a handful of shorter workings that turn back at Willesden Green and Wembley Park northbound and North Greenwich eastbound. There are also facilities to turn trains at Canary Wharf, London Bridge, Waterloo, Green Park (via the disused Charing Cross platforms), Finchley Road and West Hampstead at times of disruption.

First Trains

Northbound (Mon-Sat):	0515 Stratford to Stanmore
Southbound (Mon-Sat):	0505 Wembley Park to Stratford
Northbound (Sun):	0709 Stratford to Stanmore
Southbound (Sun):	0653 Stanmore to Stratford

Last Trains

Northbound (Mon-Sat):	0011 Stratford to Stanmore (0109)
Southbound (Mon-Sat):	0013 Stanmore to Stratford (0111)
Northbound (Sun):	2337 Stratford to Stanmore (0034)
Southbound (Sun):	2326 Stanmore to Stratford (0025)

(From September 2015, the entire line will operate a 24 hour service on Fridays and Saturdays)

With DM 96006 leading, a westbound train passes alongside Star Lane DLR station on 8 June 2013.

Notes

NORTHERN LINE →

OVERVIEW

Route: Morden to Edgware, High Barnet and Mill Hill East via Charing Cross or Bank
Type of route / operation: Tube / automatic
First section opened: Stockwell to King William Street opened by the City & South London Railway on 18 December 1890
Route mileage: 36 miles
Number of stations: 50
Trains: 1995 Tube Stock (max of 96 trains required at peak times)
Depot(s): Golders Green and Morden
Stabling points: Edgware / High Barnet / Highgate

HISTORY

The City & South London Railway was formally opened by the Prince of Wales (later to become King Edward VII) on 4 November 1890. It was to be the 18th December however, before it opened to the public. The first section opened was between Stockwell and King William Street, and this was the world's first deep level tube railway. An extension to the north opened to Moorgate Street (now Moorgate) which opened on 25 February 1900, and this involved the bypassing of the King William Street terminus which closed (parts of it are still there). An extension at the south end of the line to Clapham Common opened on 3 June 1900, with a further northern extension to Angel opening the following year on 17 November 1901. On 12 May 1907, a further northern extension opened, this time as far as Euston.

On 22 June 1907, another company known as the Charing Cross, Euston & Hampstead Railway opened a line from Charing Cross to Camden Town, where the line split with one branch going to Golders Green and the other going to what we now know as Archway, but which was called Highgate when opened. This line became known as the 'Hampstead Tube'. The CCE&HR extended to Charing Cross (Embankment) on 6 April 1914, and trains turned round here on a balloon shaped loop with no need for the driver to change ends before heading back north.

After the 1914-1918 war had ended, the City & South London Railway set about enlarging the diameter of its tunnels. Being the first deep level tube line, it had been built with smaller diameter tunnels than other lines. The north end of the line was then extended to Camden Town where it joined up with the 'Hampstead Tube', and this section opened on 20 April 1924. An extension beyond Golders Green to Edgware was also opened in stages during 1923 and 1924. At the south end, the C&SLR was extended to Morden and this opened on 13 September 1926. On the same day, an extension to the south end of the CCE&HR from Charing Cross (Embankment) saw the CCE&HR join up with the C&SLR at Kennington. This extension saw the abandonment of the balloon loop at Charing Cross (Embankment) in favour of a more standard two track, two platform arrangement.

The 1935-40 New Works Programme saw the extension of the Highgate branch to East Finchley which opened on the 3 July 1939. From there the Underground took over the LNER tracks to High Barnet, with tube trains working through from 14 April 1940. The Northern also took over the former LNER Edgware branch which diverged from the High Barnet line at Finchley Central, but it only took over the section to the first station at Mill Hill East. The main purpose of this was to serve the Mill Hill Barracks. The line beyond Mill Hill East was never electrified and was in use for freight traffic until closure in 1964.

THE ROUTE (MORDEN TO CAMDEN TOWN)

Morden

South of the station, the line continues for a short distance to Morden depot, one of two main depots on the Northern Line. The depot is the most southerly location on the entire London Underground. The station building at Morden is a Charles Holden design in Portland stone, but with the development of surrounding buildings, the front of the station is now visible. The station has three tracks, but with platform faces on both sides of two of the tracks, there are five platforms. Just a short distance from the end of the platforms, the trains go into tunnel, the first section is cut and cover, but after a short distance the train enters tube tunnel. If a train is travelling to the High Barnet branch via Bank, it will be in tunnel for 17.25 miles until it emerges into daylight at East Finchley, the longest continuous tunnel on the Underground.

South Wimbledon

This station is not actually in Wimbledon, it is in Merton and was originally named South Wimbledon (Merton). The station building is another fine Charles Holden Portland stone building, but being on a street corner is built with a curved front.

Colliers Wood

Despite the station buildings on this section of line all being designed by Charles Holden and built from Portland stone, they are all different, this one being built on a street corner like South Wimbledon, but being angular rather than curved.

Tooting Broadway

South of the platforms there is a centre reversing siding which is only used at times of disruption to turn southbound trains back north. The station has yet another fine Charles Holden building, but the site on which it was built used to be a Bank, and the safe door is still in situ as it was too heavy to remove. It is in the escalator machinery room and is sadly not visible to the public.

Tooting Bec

This station boasts two entrances one on each side of a busy crossroads. Both buildings are Charles Holden Portland stone buildings, and the smaller of the two, a subway entrance on the south side of the road, is a three sided building which has a glazed roundel on each of the three sides. Until October 1950, this station was named Trinity Road (Tooting Bec).

Balham

This station was the scene of a tragic event during the Second World War. A German bomb fell on the road above the northbound platform and a bus crashed into the crater. The tunnel partly collapsed and was filled with water from a broken water main. Over 60 people who were in the station at the time were killed and a memorial plaque is mounted on the wall of the ticket office. Interchange is available here with Network Rail's Brighton Line via a short walk of less than 100 yards.

Clapham South

This is the first station on the 1926 Morden extension and like all the other stations on the extension, has a station building finished in Portland stone and designed by Charles Holden. The station is situated on the southern edge of Clapham Common.

Clapham Common

When opened in 1900, this station was the southern terminus of the C&SLR until the Morden extension opened in 1926. The station still retains the C&SLR style island platform arrangement (see photo on page 28).

Clapham North

As per Clapham Common, this station retains a central island platform. Opened in 1900 as Clapham Road, the station got its current name when the Morden extension opened in 1926.

Clapham Common, one of two stations that still retain the City & South London Railway style of island platform. 51634 is seen heading for Morden on 10 May 2014.

Stockwell

This was the original southern terminus of the City & South London Railway until 1900 when the line was extended to Clapham Common. The site of the original station was slightly to the north of the current platforms. In line with the opening of the Victoria Line here in July 1971, the station buildings were replaced with modern structures and cross platform interchanges were provided between the two lines. If travelling north from Morden, this is the first interchange between the Northern and any other Underground line. Just north of the station, a tunnel branches off which used to serve the Stockwell works and depot. Trains used to reach this via a steep incline and were hauled up by cable. This was later replaced by a hydraulic lift. The depot was finally taken out of use in 1924.

Oval

This station takes its name from the nearby cricket ground, and when opened was called "The Oval". It was sometimes called "Kennington Oval" between 1890 and 1894, and became just "Oval" c.1894. The station building dates from the 1920s, but a recent refurbishment has given it a very modern appearance.

Kennington

At street level, Kennington is the only former City & South London Railway station to retain its original buildings, which includes a fine dome over the lift shaft. Kennington is also the junction where the two branches through central London (the Bank branch and the Charing Cross branch) meet. Only a few trains from the Charing Cross branch go through to Morden, the rest turn back using a balloon shaped loop which reverses them without the need for the driver to change ends. There is also a reversing siding which can serve either branch. Passengers arriving on a terminating train can change platform for onward travel towards Morden.

via Charing Cross (see page 30)

Elephant & Castle

The first station north of Kennington on the Bank branch is Elephant & Castle where there is interchange available with the Bakerloo Line and also with National Rail services via a short walk.

Borough

This is the most northerly of the original C&SLR stations, as the next stop heading north would have been the now disused King William Street when the line opened. Just to the south of the station, the tunnels roll over each other so that trains run on the right. The tunnels roll back over to left hand running just to the north of Bank station.

London Bridge

This station gives interchange between the Northern and the Jubilee lines as well as with the National Rail station above. The southbound Northern Line tunnel was built in 1989 and track diverted into it. The space occupied by the former southbound platform was then used to create room for additional escalators and to improve passenger flow. After London Bridge, the line passes beneath the River Thames.

Bank

A very busy interchange directly beneath the area occupied by the Bank of England. Interchange is available here with the Central Line, Waterloo & City Line, DLR and also with the Circle and District lines at nearby Monument station which is linked into the Bank complex. Above ground, a statue of James Henry Greathead (inventor of the Greathead Shield) stands outside the Royal Exchange on a plinth which covers over a ventilation shaft.

Moorgate

Interchange is available here with the Metropolitan, Hammersmith & City and Circle lines and also with the former Great Northern & City Railway, now part of Network Rail with services running from here to Stevenage and Welwyn Garden City.

Old Street

Once again, there is interchange here with the former GN&CR which has run parallel with the Northern, albeit at a different level since Moorgate. Shortly after leaving Old Street northbound, the Northern Line turns to the west and then passes through the disused City Road station which closed in 1922.

Angel

Until the early 1990s, this station had a central island platform like Clapham Common and Clapham North. The station received a major upgrade, part of which saw the northbound line diverted into a new tunnel and the space formerly occupied by the northbound line filled in creating an extra wide platform on the southbound track. Angel was the terminus of the C&SLR from 1901 until 1907.

King's Cross St Pancras

Another major hub in the Underground system, the Northern interchanges with the Victoria, Piccadilly, Hammersmith & City, Circle and Metropolitan lines of the Underground in addition to the two terminal stations of King's Cross and St Pancras, the latter offering international services to continental Europe.

Euston (City)

Shortly after leaving King's Cross towards Euston, a line comes in from the Piccadilly Line. This is where engineering trains from Ruislip depot gain access to the Northern. On the approach to Euston, northbound trains will turn left into the platform, but there is a line continuing straight ahead which connects with the southbound Northern. This is known as the Euston loop and used to be the northbound Northern Line which ran through another C&SLR style central island platform. During the late 1960s, this station was remodelled to accommodate the Victoria Line, and the northbound Northern diverted into a new tunnel. Like Angel several years later, the original position of the northbound line has been filled in giving the southbound Northern Line an unusually wide platform. The Euston loop is now used by engineering trains to gain access to and from the southbound Northern Line. The Victoria Line platforms were driven between the northbound and southbound Northern Line platforms giving cross platform interchange between the two lines. Both lines are north to south, but as Euston lies in an east to west axis, the two lines actually pass through in opposite directions, with the northbound Victoria running west to east, and the northbound Northern running through east to west. There is no physical connection here between the two lines.

The southbound platform at Euston (City) showing the wide platform created by the filling in of the former northbound track when it was diverted into a new tunnel to allow cross platform interchange with the Victoria Line in the 1960s. 51723 is arriving with a service for Angel during the period when the TBTC was being tested (the train would continue to Oval out of service, then run in service from there to Morden). 18 January 2014.

From Kennington via Charing Cross (see below)

Camden Town
Shortly after leaving Euston, the Bank branch crosses over the Charing Cross branch as it turns to the north towards Camden Town. On the approach to Camden Town there is a complex junction where trains from either Charing Cross or Bank can access either the Edgware or High Barnet branches and vice versa.

Edgware branch (see page 33)

High Barnet branch (see pages 31/32)

KENNINGTON TO CAMDEN TOWN VIA CHARING CROSS

Bank branch (see pages 28/29)

Waterloo
The first stop on the Charing Cross branch after leaving Kennington is the very busy Waterloo hub. Here there is interchange with the Waterloo & City, Bakerloo and Jubilee lines as well as the mainline terminus above. Heading north from Waterloo, the Northern passes beneath the River Thames.

Embankment
Situated at the Embankment end of Charing Cross mainline station, Embankment Underground station is served by the Bakerloo and Northern at deep level and by the Circle and District at sub surface level. Interchange is available between all lines. The station was opened as Charing Cross (Embankment) in 1914 and was renamed Charing Cross in 1915. The original name was regained in 1974, but became just Embankment in 1976. Listen out for the old style 'Mind the Gap' announcements on the northbound platform. These were recorded by Oswald Laurence

and used to be heard at many stations across the Underground. They have since been phased out, but have been restored to use at Embankment so that his widow can still hear his voice whenever she passes through the station.

When opened, this station was the southern terminus of the CCE&HR and consisted of a single platform on a balloon shaped loop. In preparation for the extension south of here, the original platform became the northbound platform, and a new southbound platform was constructed. The southbound platform dating from 1925 is straight, whereas the 1914 built northbound platform was originally on part of the balloon shaped loop and is curved.

Charing Cross

This station was opened as Charing Cross in June 1907 but was renamed to Charing Cross (Strand) in 1914 and then to just Strand in 1915. It kept this name until 1973 when the station was closed to allow the Jubilee Line Charing Cross terminus to be built. The Northern Line platforms re-opened with a new interchange with the Bakerloo and the new Jubilee Line on 1 May 1979, with the whole interchange being named Charing Cross. The Northern Line platform walls are decorated with murals painted by David Gentleman depicting the building of the Charing Cross.

Leicester Square

The rather busy Leicester Square station has entrances designed by both Charles Holden and Leslie Green. Interchange is available here with the Piccadilly Line.

Tottenham Court Road

Usually a busy interchange between the Northern and the Central lines, the station will spend much of 2015 with no Central Line service due to ongoing construction works in association with Crossrail.

Goodge Street

This 1907 station still boasts its original station building at street level which was built with a red tile facade and was designed by Leslie Green.

Warren Street

Opened as 'Euston Road', the southbound Northern Line platform still bears this name in the wall tiles. Interchange is available here with the Victoria Line.

Euston

The Northern has two stations at Euston, one on each branch. It is possible to change between the two here and also with the Victoria Line and the mainline terminus above.

Mornington Crescent

Another station that still retains its fine Leslie Green designed red tiled station building at street level. The station was closed from October 1992 until April 1998 for lift replacement work to take place. At one time it was feared the station would close for good, but thankfully that did not happen.

Camden Town

A northbound train approaching Camden Town from either of the central London branches can access both the Edgware and High Barnet branches and vice versa.

Edgware Branch (see page 33)

CAMDEN TOWN TO MILL HILL EAST AND HIGH BARNET

Kentish Town

Shortly after leaving Camden Town on the High Barnet branch, the disused South Kentish Town station is passed. This station closed in 1924 after just 17 years of service. The station building still exists at street level. The next station is Kentish Town, and this opened with the line on 22

June 1907. This is another of the former CCE&HR stations that still boasts a Leslie Green designed station building. Interchange is available with Network Rail Thameslink services.

Tufnell Park

This station boasts a delightful three sided station building that is built on the corner of the street. Like other stations on the former CCE&HR, it is a Leslie Green designed red tiled building.

Archway

Archway was the original terminus of the CCE&HR, but back then it was called Highgate. It was the terminus until the line was extended to join the LNER at East Finchley on 3 July 1939. When the next station opened on 19 January 1941, it was called Highgate and this station changed its name to Archway. There is a centre reversing siding to the north of the platforms at Archway which can be used to turn back trains from the south, although this is only used at times of service disruption.

Highgate

This station has a low level station and an abandoned high level station. Interchange between the high level and low level stations was available from 19 January 1941 until British Railways closed the high level station on 3 July 1954. Highgate station is unusual in that it has longer platforms than the trains that serve it. This came about as part of a plan to ease overcrowding when some 9 car trains were introduced (the normal length at that time being 7 cars). The platforms here and at Golders Green on the Edgware branch were long enough to accept all 9 cars and the rear two cars were used only by people travelling to Tottenham Court Road. At each station, the rear two cars would remain in the tunnels, but at Tottenham Court Road the train would draw forward to allow the passengers to alight from the rear two cars.

East Finchley

The line now climbs out of tube tunnel and into daylight and joins the former LNER line at East Finchley. The station has four platforms, the centre two being on the former LNER line to Finsbury Park and now used by empty trains running to and from Highgate sidings. The station buildings were designed by Charles Holden and include a kneeling archer firing an arrow towards central London above platform 4. To the north of the station, a Great Northern Railway signal box still exists, although out of use and boarded up.

Finchley Central

With typical Great Northern Railway station buildings, this station is the junction with the branch to Mill Hill East. There are three platforms with platform 1 only being used by trains on the Mill Hill East branch. There is a turn back siding at each end of the station. This station was actually opened many years before Underground trains came here, being built by the Edgware, Highgate & London Railway (later to become part of the Great Northern Railway) and was opened with the branch to Edgware on 22 August 1867.

Mill Hill East

Shortly after leaving Finchley Central, the branch becomes single track and there are no further points on the branch. The trackbed and bridges were built to accommodate a second track to be added as traffic developed, which it never did. This used to be a through route to Edgware, and although it was proposed to project tube trains through to Edgware, this never happened and the line was only electrified as far as Mill Hill East. LNER passenger services ceased in September 1939, with Northern Line trains running to Mill Hill East from 18 May 1941. Freight continued until 1964, after which the track beyond Mill Hill East was lifted. One of the greatest features on the branch is the Dollis Brook viaduct which stands 60 feet above the ground and is the highest point above ground on the entire Underground. The station at Mill Hill East is a single platform affair with only one track.

West Finchley

The High Barnet branch was opened after the Edgware branch, on 1st April 1872. This station was opened much later though, by the LNER in 1933.

Woodside Park

Opened with the line in 1872 as Torrington Park, the station got its current name in 1882. The station buildings are of GNR design and there is a GNR signalbox still standing at the north end of the northbound platform. The area now occupied by a car park used to be a goods yard, and BR freight trains served the goods yards here and at High Barnet, Finchley Central, East Finchley and Totteridge & Whetstone long after tube trains took over, with the last one running in 1962.

Totteridge & Whetstone

Another station with Great Northern Railway designed station buildings both at street level and at platform level.

High Barnet

This station has three platforms and a set of sidings for stabling trains when out of service. The station buildings are of GNR design and a GNR signal box still stands (disused) at the south end of platform 1.

51516 at High Barnet waiting to work a service to Morden on 10 January 2015. Note the ex GNR signal box on the left of the picture.

CAMDEN TOWN TO EDGWARE

Camden Town

Northbound trains towards Edgware use platform 1, with southbound trains coming from Edgware using platform 2. Platforms 3 and 4 cover the High Barnet branch.

High Barnet branch (see page 31/32)

Chalk Farm

This station boasts a very fine example of a Leslie Green designed red tile clad station building which takes on the shape of the road intersection on which it sits.

Belsize Park

Another station with a fine Leslie Green building. The platforms are accessed by three lifts which go down a distance of 33 metres. Or alternatively, passengers can use the 219 steps down to platform level.

Hampstead

Another station with a Leslie Green station building. If you thought Belsize Park was deep, it really was just the warm up act for the deepest station below ground on the entire Underground at Hampstead. The platforms are 58.5 metres below the surface. Lifts take passengers down to platform level, or the alternative is the staircase which has 320 steps! The depth of the station below ground is more to do with the ground going up than the tube tunnels burrowing deeper, as the line emerges into daylight before the next station at Golders Green. The station was originally going to be called Heath Street and tiles on the platform walls that have recently been restored show this proposed name.

Golders Green

Before reaching Golders Green and emerging into daylight, there is a disused station called North End. It was built but never opened. More commonly known as 'Bull & Bush' station, had it opened, it would have been the deepest on the Underground at 67 metres below the surface. Out into the open at Golders Green and there are three tunnel mouths, one northbound, one southbound and one which is just a shunt neck for Golders Green depot and is only one car long. One of two main depots on the Northern, Golders Green depot is situated alongside the station. There are three tracks through the station, but with two of the tracks having platform faces on both sides, there are five platforms. The station opened on 22 June 1907 and was the terminus of the line until the extension to Edgware opened in stages in 1923/1924.

Brent Cross

Opened as Brent in November 1923, the station has a building designed by Stanley Heaps. It was renamed to Brent Cross in 1976 when the shopping centre of that name opened nearby. The station has an island platform and immediately north of this the line goes out onto a viaduct which takes it across the North Circular Road and the River Brent.

Hendon Central

This was the temporary terminus of the Edgware branch from 19 November 1923 until 18 August 1924. At the north end of the station, the line goes back into tube tunnel. This is known as Burroughs Tunnel and it takes the line beneath the M1 motorway and the Midland Main Line.

Colindale

This station has a modern building that was built in 1962. The original station building was destroyed on 25 September 1940 when the station was hit during a German air raid. Thirteen people lost their lives and a memorial plaque was unveiled at the station in 2012. To the north of the platforms is a reversing siding, which tends to be used only at times of service disruption these days, although there is an empty train booked to reverse here at the start of traffic.

Burnt Oak

This station was not complete when the line to Edgware opened on 18 August 1924, and did not open until 27 October. It was originally called Burnt Oak (Watling), with the name becoming just Burnt Oak in the 1950s.

Edgware

The terminus at Edgware has a three track layout, part of which is covered by a train shed. The station building was designed by Stanley Heaps and today forms an interchange between the Northern Line and local bus services. A fan of sidings alongside the station provides stabling for trains outside of traffic hours.

OPERATIONS

The Northern Line is operated by a fleet of 1995 Stock trains. Since 1 June 2014, the entire line has been worked automatically using the Transmission Based Train Control (TBTC) 'moving block' system. This has eradicated all of the conventional signalling and associated train stops. Trains can be driven manually using a mode called 'Protective Manual', but for the most part they operate automatically with the Train Operator working the doors and pressing start buttons to set the train in motion.

The Mill Hill East branch is worked as a shuttle to and from Finchley Central with a few trains working to and from central London during the peak periods. Both southbound and northbound trains can work over either branch through central London and are usually listed as 'via Charing Cross' or 'via Bank' on the front of trains and on dot matrix indicators where necessary. Many of the trains that operate on the Charing Cross branch turn at Kennington with trains via Bank usually working to and from Morden. There are exceptions, and some trains via Charing Cross run to and from Morden during the peaks.

First trains:

Northbound (Mon-Sat):	0515 Morden to High Barnet via Charing Cross
Southbound (Mon-Sat):	0522 Edgware to Morden via Charing Cross and 0522 High Barnet to Morden via Bank
Northbound (Sun):	0656 Morden to High Barnet via Bank
Southbound (Sun):	0654 High Barnet to Kennington via Charing Cross

Last Trains

Northbound (Mon-Sat):	0005 Morden to High Barnet via Bank (0115)
Southbound (Mon-Sat):	0000 High Barnet to Morden via Bank
Northbound (Sun):	2310 Morden to High Barnet via Bank (0019)
Southbound (Sun):	2308 High Barnet to Morden via Bank (0019)

(From September 2015, High Barnet and Edgware to Morden via Charing Cross will operate a 24 hour service on Fridays and Saturdays)

Notes

CENTRAL LINE →

OVERVIEW
Route: West Ruislip / Ealing Broadway to Epping / Hainault / Woodford
Type of route / operation: Tube / automatic
First section opened: Shepherd's Bush to Bank opened to the public by the Central London Railway on 30 July 1900
Route mileage: 46 miles
Number of stations: 49
Trains: 1992 Tube Stock (max of 79 trains required at peak times)
Depot(s): Ruislip / Hainault
Stabling points: White City / Loughton / Woodford

HISTORY
The Central Line started life as the Central London Railway when it opened between Shepherd's Bush and Bank. The line was officially opened on 27 June 1900 by the Prince of Wales, but the public opening was over a month later on 30 July. Initially, the line was operated with electric locomotives, but the time taken to turn round at termini and the vibrations that these machines caused on the surface saw them replaced by motor carriages in 1903. In 1908, the line was extended from Shepherd's Bush to Wood Lane to serve a Franco British exhibition that was taking place there. Wood Lane station was on a balloon loop, with trains being turned for their journey back towards Bank without the need for the driver to change ends. In 1912, the east end of the line was extended from Bank to Liverpool Street. A further extension at the west end over the Great Western Railway's Ealing & Shepherd's Bush Railway to Ealing Broadway in 1920 saw trains coming off the Wood Lane loop on the right hand side, a situation that still exists today and right hand running can be witnessed around White City station. A flyover alongside Wormwood Scrubs prison switches the tracks back to left hand running.

In 1935, the 'New Works Programme' was announced and this included plans to extend the Central Line at both ends. At the west end, a new line diverged from the Ealing Broadway line near North Acton and after being delayed by the war, opened in stages, initially to Greenford in 1947, followed by West Ruislip on 21 November 1948. At the east end, the Central was to be extended to Epping and would take over LNER tracks with new sections of tunnel between Liverpool Street and Stratford, Stratford and Leyton and between Leytonstone and Newbury Park. At the outbreak of war in 1939, the tunnel section between Leytonstone and Newbury Park was structurally complete and was put into use as a secret underground aircraft components factory. Some of the other partly completed tube stations were used as air raid shelters, and Bethnal Green was the scene of a horrific tragedy that saw 173 people lose their lives. After the war, work resumed on the extension and the first section to open was Liverpool Street to Stratford on 4 December 1946. The next section to Leytonstone was opened to Central Line trains on 5 May 1947. Part of this section actually pre-dates the entire Underground, having been opened by the Eastern Counties Railway on 22 August 1856. The tunnel section to Newbury Park and the direct route to Woodford was handed over to the Central Line on 14 December 1947 with the Newbury Park to Hainault section following suit on 31 May 1948. The line north of Woodford was handed over to the Central in stages with tube trains eventually reaching Epping from 25 September 1949. Beyond Epping, the Ongar branch was taken over by London Transport, but as it was not electrified at first, British Railways steam locomotives and stock operated a shuttle service over the branch until the line was eventually electrified in 1957.

The Ongar branch was closed by London Transport on 30 September 1994 with Epping becoming the end of the Central Line from that date. Thankfully, the Ongar branch has survived and is now a flourishing preserved railway (eorailway.co.uk), and 2014 even saw an underground train (loco-hauled) work through Epping and onto the Ongar branch for the first time in 20 years.

A train of 1992 Stock led by 91235 arrives in platform 2 at Epping on 30 November 2013. This is the eastern terminus of the Central Line, although the former Ongar branch survives and is still physically connected at the end of the platforms.

THE ROUTE (EPPING TO LEYTONSTONE)

Epping

The end of the Central Line since 1994 when the Ongar branch closed. At the east end of the platforms will be seen the stop lights preventing further travel, although it will be noted that the track is still in place onto the Ongar branch which is now a preserved railway. In 2014, the visit of the preserved Cravens 1960 Stock set to the Epping & Ongar Railway saw the stop lights removed at the end of platform 1 to allow the train to continue to North Weald (hauled by Schöma diesel locos as the Ongar branch is no longer electrified). In November 2014, several engineering trains passed through onto the Ongar branch during engineering work in and around Epping station. When the E&OR is operating, look out for vintage buses that call at the front of Epping station to take people to North Weald where they can board a train on the Ongar branch.

To the south of the station is Epping signal cabin. This is currently owned by the Cravens Heritage Trust, and in front of the cabin on a plinth is electric locomotive L11 which is undergoing restoration. This loco was made from two Standard Stock driving motors to make one vehicle with a cab at each end, and was used in this form as a shunter at Acton Works. Epping is the only station served by tube trains to be outside the M25 London Orbital Motorway (the sub surface Metropolitan Line also goes outside the M25). The Central Line passes under the M25 about 3/4 mile south of Epping.

Theydon Bois

Theydon Bois is a quiet Essex village which first had a railway station when the Great Eastern Railway reached there on 24 April 1865.

Debden

Initially called Chigwell Road when opened by the GER in 1865, it was soon renamed Chigwell Lane and did not become Debden until the Central Line took over in 1949. To the north of the platforms is a central reversing siding which is used to reverse a few trains during peak hours.

Loughton

This is a three track station with four platforms (the central track has a platform face on both sides). Some trains from central London reverse here on the central track (platforms 2 and 3). To the south of the station is a set of sidings where about ten trains are stabled overnight. The station itself was designed by John Murray Easton and is a grade II listed building. The station platforms have sleek looking reinforced concrete canopies and wooden benches with roundel nameboards as seat backs.

Buckhurst Hill

The station buildings here date from 1892, although the station was actually opened by the Eastern Counties Railway in 1856.

Hainault loop (see pages 39/40)

Woodford

Roughly 3/4 mile to the north of Woodford is Woodford Junction where the Hainault loop branches off. Woodford station has three platforms, platform 1 being a dead end bay. Alongside platform 1 are 5 sidings which are used to stable trains outside traffic hours. To the south of the station is a reversing siding which is used to reverse trains that have arrived via the Hainault loop and terminated at Woodford, although it is also possible to reverse a train in the platform.

South Woodford

Opened in August 1856 as South Woodford (George Lane), the suffix was dropped when the Central Line took over in 1947 but, unusually, the suffix has been kept on the roundel nameboards on the platform. There used to be a level crossing at the Woodford end of the station which was removed when the line was electrified. There is an entrance on either side of the line and the footbridge linking the two platforms is outside the ticket gates. There is also a pedestrian subway beneath the line to the north of the platforms linking the two halves of George Lane.

Snaresbrook

Snaresbrook station still retains a lot of its 19th century features including ornate canopy brackets and Victorian station building. The concrete roundels which incorporate station lamps are a later London Transport addition.

Hainault loop (see pages 39/40)

One of many mosaics that line the walls of the subway at Leytonstone depicting scenes from films directed by Leytonstone born Alfred Hitchcock. This particular mosaic shows a scene from the 1940 psychological drama 'Rebecca'.
It is worth breaking your journey here to view the mosaics which were created by the Greenwich Mural workshop.

To the north of Leytonstone, the Epping line passes through Whipps Cross Tunnel and then the line from Newbury Park (the southern half of the Hainault loop) rises up from tube tunnel and joins the Epping line. There are three platforms at Leytonstone which are reached by a subway which also forms a public footpath beneath the railway. The subway is decorated with mosaics depicting scenes from films by Leytonstone born film director Alfred Hitchcock.

LEYTONSTONE TO WOODFORD VIA THE HAINAULT LOOP

Leytonstone

Wanstead

The Hainault loop (sometimes also called the Chigwell loop) dives down into tube tunnel to the north of Leytonstone station and the first station is at Wanstead. At the start of the war, this section of tunnel had been built but had not had tracks and other fixtures and fittings installed. It was used as a secret underground aircraft components factory which was operated by the Plessey Company. The factory was long and included all three of the current stations on this section. Due to its length, materials were moved between sections of the factory using an 18 inch gauge tramway.

Redbridge

This station is a mere 17 feet below ground, and was built by the cut and cover method with the tracks diving down into tube tunnels at either end. It consists of a central island platform.

Gants Hill

Designer Charles Holden designed this station with a large circulating area between the platforms with a barrel vaulted ceiling in a similar style to Moscow Metro stations. Art deco uplighters give this area a stylish finish.

Newbury Park

Emerging into daylight on the approach to Newbury Park, the line joins the formation of what used to be the Great Eastern Railway's Ilford to Woodford via Hainault line. The station still retains a lot of GER features. Connection can be made here with a number of local bus services that call at the adjacent bus station which is a grade II listed building with a copper covered barrel vaulted roof. North of the platform there is a central reversing siding which is accessed at the south end, but can also be exited at the north end. The siding is used by regular trains that are booked to reverse here.

The delightful Gants Hill station on the Hainault loop with its Moscow Metro style central circulating area between the platforms, complete with barrel vaulted ceiling.
This view is taken from the west end of the circulating area looking towards the escalators.

Barkingside
Opened by the GER in May 1903, the station is largely untouched and is now a grade II listed building.

Fairlop
Opened on the same day as Barkingside, Fairlop is another station that retains many GER features.

Hainault
A three platform station with most trains terminating here and working back towards Newbury Park. Some trains do work through however to serve the top half of the Hainault loop to Woodford. To the north of the station is Hainault depot, one of two main depots on the Central Line.

Grange Hill
Situated at the far end of Hainault depot, some trains start and terminate here at the beginning and end of traffic hours and run into depot. The station is largely to a GER design with the exception of the ticket office which was destroyed by a V1 flying bomb during World War II. On the Woodford side of the station is Mount Pleasant Tunnel which is to standard height as it was built when the line was part of the GER.

Chigwell
This station is a GER gem, which unlike Grange Hill, still retains its original GER station building.

Roding Valley
This station is situated very close to the junction with the line to and from Epping visible from the platforms here. This is officially the least used station on the Underground with an average of less than 600 passengers per day.

Woodford

LEYTONSTONE TO WEST RUISLIP

Leyton
Opened by the Eastern Counties Railway on 22 August 1856 as Low Leyton, it was renamed to Leyton in 1868. The station today largely dates from 1879. To the south of the station, the line goes into tube tunnel alongside the south end of the Temple Mills Eurostar depot.

Stratford
The Central Line is in tube tunnel at either end of Stratford station but climbs to the surface to serve platforms 3 and 3a (westbound) and platform 6 (eastbound). Trains heading west open their doors on both sides here. Stratford is a large transport hub and connection can be made with Network Rail, London Overground, Docklands Light Railway, the Jubilee Line and local bus services. This station also serves the nearby Westfield shopping centre and the Olympic Park. If heading west, the line dives down into tube tunnel and daylight will not be seen again until White City.

Mile End
The Central Line tracks serve the outer faces of two island platforms with the tracks of the District and Hammersmith & City in the middle. This is the only place on the Underground where cross platform interchange between a tube line and a sub surface line takes place below the ground.

Bethnal Green
At the start of the war, this station was partly complete and was used as an air raid shelter. It was the scene of a terrible tragedy on the night of 3 March 1943. It is believed that a new type of anti-aircraft rocket was launched from the nearby Victoria Park, and that this caused people to panic, believing it to be a German attack. A crowd ran to Bethnal Green tube station for shelter, and a

The 'Stairway to Heaven' memorial in Bethnal Green Gardens. An inverted skyward bound stairway remains to be fitted to the top of the plinth seen in the picture.

person, believed to be a lady carrying a child, tripped and fell on the stairs. Very quickly, approximately 300 people became crushed into the small stairwell and 173 people lost their lives mostly through suffocation. A small plaque commemorates this tragedy above one of the station entrances. A larger memorial is now in place alongside the entrance in the adjacent Bethnal Green Gardens, although not yet quite complete.

Liverpool Street

As well as serving the mainline terminus above ground, there is also interchange here with the Hammersmith & City, Circle and Metropolitan lines. A pair of reversing sidings are situated at the east end of the station, used only at times of disruption nowadays.

Bank

There are some sharp curves around Bank including through the platforms themselves. This is to follow the roads above, but also at one point, to avoid the vaults of the Bank of England. This was the original eastern terminus of the Central London Railway, but today is a through station which interchanges with the Waterloo & City Line, Northern Line, Docklands Light Railway and also with the District and Circle lines at the nearby Monument station.

St Paul's

Originally called 'Post Office' when opened in 1900. It is believed that the name was chosen to differentiate it from the nearby South Eastern Railway station called St Paul's, but when this was renamed Blackfriars in 1937, the Underground station took the name St Paul's. As the name would suggest, this station is conveniently located for St Paul's Cathedral. The westbound tunnel is situated over the eastbound tunnel here.

Chancery Lane

In a reverse of St Paul's, the eastbound tunnel is situated above the westbound tunnel here. This means that there is a steady climb from Holborn, and if you stand at the west end of the eastbound platform and look into the tunnel, you can actually see the previous station at Holborn and watch your train depart there and climb all the way to Chancery Lane.

Holborn

Here there is interchange with the Piccadilly Line. Between here and Tottenham Court Road is the disused British Museum station. There is a reversing siding here for turning westbound trains back eastwards, which is currently only used at times of disruption.

Tottenham Court Road

Normally there is interchange here with the Northern Line's Charing Cross branch, but Central Line trains will not be stopping here for most of 2015 due to construction work in association with Crossrail.

Oxford Circus

A busy station serving the West End shopping district, there is also interchange with the Victoria and Bakerloo lines here.

Bond Street

In 1909, Harry Selfridge tried to get the name of this station changed to Selfridges, but this was quashed by the CLR. Today this station serves the busy shopping area and also connects with the Jubilee Line (and also eventually with Crossrail).

Marble Arch

Situated at the very western end of Oxford Street, this station is named after the nearby white marble triumphal arch. There is a reversing siding situated to the west of the station which can turn westbound trains back eastwards. It is only used at times of service disruption.

Lancaster Gate

Although not shown on the tube map, this station is located within easy walking distance of Paddington mainline station, and it is probably quicker to walk from here than change at Notting Hill Gate for the Circle and District lines to Paddington.

Queensway

Opened on 30 July 1900 as Queen's Road, it was renamed to Queensway in September 1946. The station building at street level was designed by Harry Bell Measures for the CLR. There used to be a reversing siding to the east of the stations for turning eastbound trains back west, but this has now been lifted and replaced (unusually) with a facing crossover which can be used to turn back trains at times of service disruption.

Notting Hill Gate

Here there is interchange with the District and Circle line station above. Despite the Metropolitan Railway opening what is now the District and Circle line station in 1868, and the Central London Railway opening the deep level tube station in 1900, it wasn't until 1959 that the two stations were linked, each having their own separate entrances until then.

Holland Park

This station appears to be frozen in time with tiled walls and enamel station signs along the length of the platforms.

Shepherd's Bush

The original terminus of the CLR, this has been a through station since the opening of Wood Lane in 1908. Trains heading west take the Caxton curve, the tightest curve on the Underground, and continue round part of the former Wood Lane loop before emerging on the right hand side at White City.

White City

Westbound trains emerge into daylight for the first time since Stratford. Right hand running occurs here (for reasons stated in the 'History' of the Central Line section). This station opened on 23 November 1947 and replaced Wood Lane. The design of the station won an award at the Festival of Britain, and a plaque to this effect can be seen near the main entrance. There are three tracks through the station with the centre track having a platform face on either side and used frequently for turning back trains from central London. There is also a reversing siding at the country end of the station. Between here and East Acton is a flyover which reverts the two tracks to left hand running.

East Acton

This station has GWR waiting shelters on each platform, which reflects the fact that this section of line was built by the GWR and initially the CLR only had running powers over it, sharing the tracks with GWR freight trains until an additional two tracks were added in 1938.

A picture illustrating the right hand running at White City. On the left can be seen an eastbound train showing white headlights, while on the right is a westbound train showing red tail lights. This picture was taken on 6 July 2013 with 91099 on the right and 91293 on the left.

North Acton

After passing beneath the Great Western mainline and the North London Line, the next station is North Acton. Until the line was upgraded in the 1990s, there were only two platforms on the Central Line. There are now three and the newest (platform 3) is used by eastbound trains, platform 1 is used by westbound trains and platform 2 is mostly used by trains that reverse here. A short distance to the west of North Acton is North Acton Junction where the West Ruislip line diverges from the Ealing Broadway route.

to West Ruislip (see below)

West Acton

The station building here is a brick box with glass and concrete frontage. It was designed by Brian Lewis and completed in 1940 to replace an earlier station building as part of the New Works Programme.

Ealing Broadway

The Central Line terminates here in platforms 5 and 6 in between the Network Rail platforms (1 to 4) and the District Line platforms (7 to 9). There used to be a physical connection between the Central and the District, but this has been removed.

NORTH ACTON TO WEST RUISLIP

North Acton

Hanger Lane

Situated beneath the Hanger Lane gyratory where the A40 Western Avenue meets the A406 North Circular Road, the station building here is located in the centre of the gyratory and is accessed by a number of passenger subways.

Perivale

On the approach to this station is the very attractive grade II listed former Hoover factory. Built in 1933, the building is a fine example of an art deco building. It no longer performs the function for which it was built and is now part of a supermarket, but the building still looks impressive and is best viewed from a passing Central Line train.

North Acton Junction with an eastbound train coming off the West Ruislip branch led by 91101. The two centre tracks go to Ealing Broadway, while the track on the left dives down underneath to head to West Ruislip. The track on the far right is Network Rail's Old Oak Common to Greenford line. 6 July 2013.

Greenford

This station is situated close to a Network Rail junction where the line from Old Oak Common is joined on a triangular junction by the line from West Ealing. This latter line still has a regular passenger service and trains from Paddington terminate in a bay platform between the eastbound and westbound Central Line platforms and cross platform interchange is available between the two lines on the eastbound side. Greenford was also home to the last wooden escalator on the Underground which was removed during 2014 to make way for an inclined lift.

Northolt

This location has a central reversing siding for turning back trains from central London and several trains are timetabled to reverse here. Shortly after Northolt towards West Ruislip, the Network Rail line alongside us is joined by the main Chiltern route from Marylebone to High Wycombe, Princes Risborough, Banbury and beyond.

South Ruislip

This station serves both the Central Line and the Network Rail platforms and interchange is available between the two.

Ruislip Gardens

Situated alongside RAF Northolt, this is the penultimate station on the line. Some trains start and finish their journeys here at the beginning and end of traffic hours as just to the north of the platform is the entrance to Ruislip depot, one of two main depots on the Central Line.

West Ruislip

After passing alongside the large Ruislip depot, the end of the line at West Ruislip is reached. This is an island platform affair alongside the Network Rail station and interchange is available between the two. There is also a link between Network Rail and the Underground, which is used to deliver materials to Ruislip depot (as this is the main base for engineering trains) and is also used for deliveries of new S Stock trains from Bombardier in Derby. At the back of Ruislip depot is a link with the Piccadilly and Metropolitan Uxbridge branch.

OPERATIONS

The whole of the Central Line is operated automatically using a system of ATO (Automatic Train Operation) and ATP (Automatic Train Protection). The ATO drives the train while the ATP picks up codes in the track to determine target speeds. Trains can be worked manually if necessary and are also driven manually in and out of sidings. There are still some signals on the line at the start of each block section to allow for manual operation, and these display either green, red or white. The red means stop and is applicable to all trains, green means go and is applicable to all trains, and the white means go for a train in automatic mode, but stop for a train being driven manually.

The majority of trains run between Epping and West Ruislip, Ealing Broadway and Hainault (via Newbury Park), Ealing Broadway and Woodford (via Hainault), Newbury Park and White City and between Loughton and Northolt. There are also a number of trains that reverse at Debden and North Acton during peak hours.

First trains:

Westbound (Mon-Sat):	0510 Epping to West Ruislip*
Eastbound (Mon-Sat):	0523 West Ruislip to Epping
Westbound (Sun):	0642 Epping to West Ruislip*
Eastbound (Sun):	0641 West Ruislip to Epping

Last trains:

Westbound (Mon-Sat):	2345 Epping to West Ruislip (0110)
Eastbound (Mon-Sat):	2353 West Ruislip to Epping (0116)*
Westbound (Sun):	2257 Epping to West Ruislip (0028)
Eastbound (Sun):	2258 West Ruislip to Epping (0022)*

(From September 2015, a 24 hour service will operate on Fridays and Saturdays from Ealing Broadway to Hainault and Loughton)

* These trains starting and finishing at Epping stable in Loughton sidings and run in service between Loughton and Epping and vice versa.

91275 leads an eastbound service into Queensway on 25 September 2014.

OVERVIEW

Route: Waterloo to Bank
Type of route / operation: Tube / manually driven with conventional signalling
First section opened: Waterloo to Bank, opened by the Waterloo & City Railway Company on
8 August 1898
Route mileage: 1.5 miles
Number of stations: 2
Trains: 1992 Tube Stock (max of 5 trains required at peak times)
Depot(s): Waterloo
Stabling points: Bank

HISTORY

The Waterloo & City Line was opened to passengers by the Waterloo & City Railway Company (part of the London & South Western Railway), on 8 August 1898, although there had been a formal opening four weeks earlier on 11 July 1898. This line was not opened in stages, as it has and always has had, only two stations. It was built to transport commuters arriving at the LSWR's Waterloo terminus into the heart of the City of London. Ownership passed from the LSWR to the Southern Railway in 1923 and then to British Railways upon nationalisation in 1948. It remained a part of British Rail (latterly under the Network Southeast banner) until it was sold to London Underground in 1994. It was also converted from the Southern's third rail system to the standard LU four rail system to coincide with the introduction of new trains (class 482) towards the end of BR's ownership of the line. It is worth noting that at both Waterloo and Bank, the old BR Network Southeast branding can still be seen under the yellow line on the edge of the platforms.

THE ROUTE (WATERLOO TO BANK)

Waterloo

Trains arriving from Bank arrive in the set down only platform 26 and detrain. They then proceed into the depot where they reverse and come out into the pick up only platform 25 and form a train to Bank. Shortly after leaving Waterloo, if you are eagle eyed, you will spot what appears to be an old junction. This is where a line used to go to a hydraulic lift where trains could be lifted out and taken away for repair. This lift was removed during the construction of the Eurostar terminal. If trains need to be removed from the line for heavy repair today, they have to be lifted out of Waterloo depot by mobile crane at the junction of Lower Marsh/Spur Road.

The line passes beneath the River Thames close to Blackfriars Bridge and then runs parallel to the District and Circle lines, albeit at a deeper level, from Blackfriars to Mansion House where it turns away from the River to the terminus at Bank.

Bank

There are two platforms and the approach to the terminus has a scissors crossover. From here there is interchange with the Central Line, Northern Line (Bank branch), Docklands Light Railway and the Circle and District lines at the nearby Monument station.

OPERATIONS

The Waterloo & City is operated by trains of 1992 Stock in four car formations. These are manually driven using conventional signalling. All trains are maintained at the depot at Waterloo, and the line is not connected to any other part of the Underground network. The main purpose of this railway is to serve the needs of commuters heading into the City of London, and for this reason it is closed on Sundays and Bank Holidays. Occasionally if the Northern Line (Bank branch) is closed for engineering work on a Sunday, the Waterloo & City may run on a Sunday.

First trains:

Eastbound (Mon-Fri):	0615 Waterloo to Bank
Westbound (Mon-Fri):	0621 Bank to Waterloo
Eastbound (Sat):	0800 Waterloo to Bank
Westbound (Sat):	0802 Bank to Waterloo

Last trains:

Eastbound (Mon-Fri):	0020 Waterloo to Bank (0025)
Westbound (Mon-Fri)	0026 Bank to Waterloo (0031)
Eastbound (Sat):	0020 Waterloo to Bank (0025)
Westbound (Sat):	0026 Bank to Waterloo (0031)

Looking from the departure platform at Waterloo (number 25) towards the depot, a train led by 65501 moves out of the depot (having just reversed) ready to form the next train to Bank. 14 December 2013

PICCADILLY LINE →

OVERVIEW
Route: Cockfosters to Heathrow and Uxbridge
Type of route / operation: Tube / manually driven with conventional signalling
First section opened: Finsbury Park to Hammersmith, opened by the Great Northern Piccadilly & Brompton Railway on 15 December 1906
Route mileage: 44.3 miles
Number of stations: 53
Trains: 1973 Tube Stock (max of 79 trains required at peak times)
Depot(s): Cockfosters / Northfields
Stabling points: Arnos Grove / South Harrow / Uxbridge

HISTORY

The Great Northern Piccadilly & Brompton Railway opened a line from Finsbury Park to Hammersmith on 15 December 1906. On 30 November 1907, a short branch from Holborn to The Strand (later renamed Aldwych) was opened.

The first extension of the line saw Piccadilly Line services going beyond Hammersmith using the centre pair of tracks between Hammersmith and Acton Town to give a non-stop service parallel to the District, an arrangement that still exists to this day. Further extensions to the west saw the Piccadilly take over lines already operated by the District. Firstly to South Harrow from 4 July 1932, and then on to Uxbridge from 23 October 1933. The Hounslow branch was also taken over with Piccadilly trains to Northfields from 9 January 1933 and to Hounslow West from 13 March 1933.

An extension to the east end of the line to Cockfosters was built in the 1930s and opened in stages between 1932 and 1933, with Cockfosters being reached on 31 July 1933.

In 1975, a new tunnel section was opened from Hounslow West towards Heathrow Airport opening to Hatton Cross on 19 July 1975, and to Heathrow Central (now renamed Heathrow Terminals 1,2,3) on 16 December 1977. The Piccadilly has since had to keep up with the expansion of the airport above, so on 12 April 1986, the Heathrow Terminal 4 station was opened on a loop, followed by a new terminus at Heathrow Terminal 5 which opened on 27 March 2008.

Just one section of the Piccadilly has succumbed to closure, this being the short branch from Holborn to Aldwych which closed on 30 September 1994 (the same day as the Central's Ongar branch). The Aldwych branch is still in situ and is used for training and filming purposes.

THE ROUTE (COCKFOSTERS TO HEATHROW)

Cockfosters
This station has a three track layout under a concrete roof designed by Charles Holden. The design of the station is very similar to that at Uxbridge at the other end of the Piccadilly. To the west of the station on the west side is Cockfosters depot, one of two main depots on the Piccadilly (the other being Northfields).

Oakwood
The next station is Oakwood, which is situated at the west end of Cockfosters depot. As a result, some trains start and finish their journeys here at the beginning and end of traffic.

Southgate

The east end of the Piccadilly is above ground with the exception of this station which is beneath a hill and is in a short section of tube tunnel. The station is unusual in that it is possible to see daylight from each end of the station platforms. The station building is a circular art deco design by Charles Holden with an illuminated 'Tesla Coil' fixed to the centre of the roof.

Arnos Grove

Some trains reverse at Arnos Grove rather than run through to Cockfosters. There are also seven sidings here where trains are stabled outside of traffic hours.

Bounds Green

To the west of Arnos Grove, the line goes into tube tunnel, and does not emerge into daylight again until the approach to Barons Court on the west side of London. Although the station building here is typical of Charles Holden, it was in fact the only station on the Cockfosters extension not to be designed by him, being the work of his colleague C.H.James instead. This station suffered bomb damage during the war when a part of the westbound platform tunnel collapsed due to heavy bombing above ground. Several people who were sheltering in the station were injured or killed and a plaque at the north end of the westbound platform remembers them.

Wood Green

This station has a turn back siding for turning back trains from central London. It is only used at times of service disruption these days. The station building is on a corner and Charles Holden designed a curved station frontage to fit the location.

Turnpike Lane

This station features yet another Holden designed station, this one being a very large brick box with concrete lid which also features two large ventilation towers.

Manor House

Of all the stations on the Cockfosters extension, this station has the plainest buildings, and indeed, the only ones which are not grade II listed on this section of the Piccadilly.

A westbound train arrives at Turnpike Lane. Note the ornate ventilation covers above the roundel.

Finsbury Park

Here there is interchange with Network Rail and with the Victoria Line. There is also a physical connection between the Piccadilly and the Victoria which is used by engineering trains to gain access to and from the Victoria Line. The Piccadilly was altered here in the 1960s to accommodate the new Victoria Line. The former Northern City Line tunnels which were built to standard height (as opposed to tube height), were taken over by the westbound Piccadilly and the southbound Victoria. The old Piccadilly westbound platform became the northbound Victoria and the eastbound Piccadilly platform remained unaltered. This does mean that the size of the overall bore of the westbound Piccadilly Line tunnel is much larger than the trains that use it (as is also the southbound Victoria Line tunnel). Also of note are the mosaics of hot air balloons on the walls, Finsbury Park being the location of one of the very first hot air balloon flights.

Above left: A rear view of a westbound departing train at Finsbury Park showing the large bore of the tunnel. *Above right:* Colour light signal at the end of the platform at Arsenal, still doing the job for which it was designed, and probably dating back to the early 20th century.

Arsenal

Originally named Gillespie Road, this station was renamed to Arsenal (Highbury Hill) in 1932 with the suffix being dropped around 1960, making it the only Underground station to be named after a football club. The original name can still be seen in the wall tiles. This station is also unusual for a tube station in that it has no lifts and no escalators. Instead there is a long sloping walkway from the entrance to the platforms, due to the platforms being not very deep below the surface and located directly beneath the East Coast Main Line.

Holloway Road

This station still retains its original Leslie Green designed station building with red tiled facade and GNP&BR lettering. Now that Arsenal Football Club have moved to their new purpose built Emirates Stadium, this station is in a better location to serve the new venue than Arsenal. The station struggles to cope with the number of people on match days however, as access to the platforms is by lift only, so the station becomes exit only close to match start time. The now disused second lift shaft here was once home to an experimental spiral escalator which was not a success and never used by the public.

Caledonian Road

Another station to retain its Leslie Green designed station building, now grade II listed (as too is the one at Holloway Road). Between here and Kings Cross there is a disused station called York Road which was closed on 17 September 1932.

King's Cross St Pancras

One of the busiest stations on the Underground serving the mainline termini of King's Cross and St Pancras. There is also interchange with the Northern (Bank branch), Victoria, Hammersmith & City, Circle and Metropolitan lines. King's Cross is remembered for the terrible fire on 18 November 1987 which claimed 31 lives and was started by discarded smoking material on one of the escalators serving the Piccadilly Line. A memorial plaque and clock remembers those who lost their lives. To the west of the station is a crossover and a branch off the eastbound track links to the Northern at Euston, the latter being used by engineering trains travelling to and from the Northern Line.

Russell Square

This station still retains its Leslie Green designed red tiled station building, and at platform level has a unique design of green and cream tiling. It is worth pointing out that the Piccadilly Line stations in the central area all had a unique tile design when built to make them identifiable to people who could not read (illiteracy was common in 1906).

Holborn

Despite the fact that the Piccadilly and Central Line cross over each other at Holborn, Park Royal and Ealing, Holborn is the only place where there is actually interchange between these two lines. Holborn is also where the now closed Aldwych branch diverges. No longer used by passenger services, London Underground use the tunnels and station at Aldwych for filming and training. A short distance from the station entrance in Southampton Row is the entrance to the former Kingsway tram subway which still has its conduit track in place. The subway is currently being used by construction workers on the Crossrail project, but the tram tracks and subway entrance can still be clearly seen.

Covent Garden

The opening of this station was delayed and it did not open until 11 April 1907 (the line through here was opened on 15 December 1906). The station still retains its Leslie Green designed red tiled station building. Access to the platforms is via lifts or a 193 step spiral staircase.

Leicester Square

Interchange with the Northern Line's Charing Cross branch is available here.

Piccadilly Circus

This station has an interchange with the Bakerloo Line. The ticket hall area is well worth exploring as it has a circular concourse and retains many late-1920s features including art deco style pillars and a linear clock which tells the time for anywhere in the world.

Green Park

Opened in 1906, it wasn't until 1969 that this station served anything other than the Piccadilly. From 1969, interchange became available with the new Victoria Line, and this was added to in 1979 when the Jubilee Line also opened through here. The station was originally named Dover Street. Between Green Park and Hyde Park Corner is the closed station called Down Street, which closed on 21 May 1932 and was subsequently used during the war by Winston Churchill, his cabinet and the Railway Executive Committee. The Leslie Green designed station building still exists at street level. To the west of the station there is a centre reversing siding that can be used to turn back westbound trains This facility is only used at times of service disruption.

Hyde Park Corner

There are no longer any surface buildings associated with this station, and it is reached via a series of pedestrian subways beneath the busy road junction. The original station building does still exist though and is currently in use as part of a hotel. It is easily distinguished by its red coloured tiles so favoured by designer Leslie Green.

Knightsbridge

Alight here for the famous Harrods department store and the fashionable shopping area around Knightsbridge. It has always been a busy station, the same of which cannot be said for the now disused Brompton Road station just to the west of Knightsbridge. It closed on 30 July 1934 due to low passenger numbers.

South Kensington

The Piccadilly now meets the District and Circle Lines, albeit at a deeper level, and interchange between the Piccadilly and the sub surface lines is possible here and at the next station.

Gloucester Road

At street level, there are two station buildings, one to serve the Piccadilly and one to serve the Circle and District. Only the latter is still used as an entrance to serve both lines. The Piccadilly station building designed by Leslie Green is still there but is now used by several retail outlets.

Earl's Court

The Piccadilly is still beneath the District at Earl's Court, but the Circle turned away at Gloucester Road. Interchange is available between the two lines with the Piccadilly platforms being directly beneath those of the District.

Barons Court

Just to the east of Barons Court, the two tracks of the Piccadilly rise up out of tube tunnel in between the eastbound and westbound tracks of the District. Cross platform interchange between the two lines is available here. Although the first tracks through here were opened in 1874 by the Metropolitan District Railway, the station was not built until 1905 and was to serve new developments in the area as well as to prepare for the arrival of the GNP&BR which opened through here one year later. The station building is of particular interest, being a grade II listed structure designed by Harry Ford and still bearing the name of the District Railway above the entrance. Old style 'light box' train describers still show the next trains on this station and there are no dot matrix indicators giving passengers a countdown to the next trains.

Hammersmith

On the east side of Hammersmith there is a centre reversing siding that can be used to turn back Piccadilly or District Line trains from either direction. Crossovers allow District and Piccadilly Line trains to swap tracks and are often used at times of disruption. Under normal operating conditions, the Piccadilly runs on the centre two of four tracks with the District on the outer tracks. On the eastbound Piccadilly track between here and Barons Court is a gantry from which are suspended three glass hoops which are painted on the inside with a conductive silver paint. Tube Stock passes beneath it, but should a full size District Line train pass under it, the hoops would be smashed which would break a circuit and throw the signals to danger and raise the associated train stops. This is to prevent a wrongly signalled District Line train from reaching the tube tunnels of the Piccadilly. The station itself is a modernised four platform affair beneath the Broadway complex and is accessed via the Broadway shopping mall. In the entrance area, part of the old station stonework has been preserved. Interchange between the Piccadilly and District is possible here, and also with trains at the nearby terminus of the Hammersmith & City and Circle lines via a short walk across Hammersmith Broadway. Heading west, the Piccadilly runs non-stop from here to Acton Town, passing through the stations at Ravenscourt Park, Stamford Brook and Chiswick Park. Piccadilly trains do call at Turnham Green, but only at the beginning and end of service each day. A description of these stations is in the District section of the book.

In the circulating area of Hammersmith station, a section of the original station building that was demolished to make way for the Hammersmith Broadway development has been restored and incorporated into one of the walls.

Acton Town

This is a four platform station situated next to the junction where the Ealing Broadway and Uxbridge branches turn away from the Heathrow branch. Cross platform interchange is available here between the Piccadilly and the District, for the first time since Hammersmith. On the east side of the station is Acton Works, where at one time most of the Underground's stock would come here for major maintenance. This work is mostly done by the line depots now and the role of the Works is reduced from what it once was. To the west of the station lies the District Line's Ealing Common depot and the Acton store of the London Transport Museum where many historic vehicles are kept, and which opens its doors to the public several times per year. Acton Town opened as Mill Hill Park on 1 July 1879 by the Metropolitan District Railway. Its name was changed to Acton Town on 1 March 1910. The station was rebuilt in 1931/32 ready for the changeover of the Uxbridge branch from the District to the Piccadilly. The station building is a typical Charles Holden design.

To the west of the station, the Heathrow branch continues straight on and then bears left with the line to Ealing Broadway and Uxbridge going over the top of the Heathrow branch. It is also possible for Heathrow branch trains to take the Uxbridge line, but before going over the top of the Heathrow branch, they can turn off and join the westbound local Piccadilly on the Heathrow branch. Trains from Ealing Broadway and Uxbridge descend on the opposite side of the Heathrow branch, and this also incorporates the exit from Ealing Common depot. The eastbound local on the Heathrow branch passes beneath the line from Ealing Broadway and Uxbridge to come alongside it on the approach to the station.

To South Harrow and Uxbridge (see page 55)

South Ealing

One of only two station names on the Underground to include all of the vowels (the other being Mansion House). There are four tracks between Acton Town and Northfields. The two centre tracks being the fast lines, and the outer tracks being the locals. The eastbound local at South Ealing also doubles up as a test track and is fitted with pipes that can spray water onto the track to simulate wet weather conditions.

53

The eastbound local line at South Ealing doubles up as a test track, and in this view, a train of Central Line 1992 Stock can be seen undergoing brake tests on 21 June 2014. The pipework for spraying the track to simulate wet weather can be clearly seen. On the left, a train of Piccadilly Line 1973 Stock heads west with a service for Heathrow.

Northfields

A four track station with a superb example of Charles Holden's design work for a station building. To the west of the station is the large Northfields depot, one of two main depots on the Piccadilly. Beyond here now the Heathrow branch is down to two tracks.

Boston Manor

Opened by the Metropolitan District Railway as Boston Road on 1 May 1883, this station still retains a District Railway signalbox at the west end of the eastbound platform, though now no longer in use, and District Railway platform buildings and canopies. The station buildings at street level date from 1934 and were designed by Stanley Heaps. Northfields depot has an exit at the west end, with trains exiting this way passing behind the platforms.

Osterley

This station was opened on 25 March 1934 to replace the former Osterley & Spring Road station, the abandoned platforms of which can still be seen from the current platforms and from passing trains. Like Boston Manor, the station buildings were designed by Stanley Heaps.

Hounslow East

There used to be a triangular junction here with the original Hounslow Town station being a terminus on one side of the triangle. The current Hounslow East station opened on 2 May 1909 as Hounslow Town on the opposite side of the triangle to replace the terminus station of the same name and prevent the need for reversing. The station was renamed to Hounslow East in 1925. The station buildings are of a modern design, having been rebuilt in 2002.

Hounslow Central

Opened as Heston & Hounslow by the Metropolitan District Railway on 1 April 1886 (the line through here had already been open since 21 July 1884). The station was renamed Hounslow Central in 1925. The station building dates from 1912.

Hounslow West

This was the terminus of the MDR's line and was opened on 21 July 1884 as Hounslow Barracks. It was renamed to Hounslow West in 1925. It remained as the terminus after the Piccadilly Line took over until the opening of the Heathrow extension. In order to accommodate the new extension, a new station had to be built on a new alignment, and the terminus closed and new station opened on the 14 July 1975. The current station is underground, although you can see daylight at the east end. The line now runs in tunnel all the way to Heathrow except for a short stretch where the line climbs to pass over the top of the River Crane which brings the line briefly out into the open. Known as Crane Bank, this is situated between Hounslow West and Hatton Cross.

Hatton Cross

The Heathrow extension opened as far as here on 19 July 1975. Then it was a terminus station, becoming a plain through station when Heathrow Central opened on 16 December 1977. Now though, there is a junction to the west of the platforms where the single track loop line towards Terminal 4 branches off.

The layout of the Heathrow loop is best explained with the help of a schematic map. Service patterns see trains for Terminal 4 branch off just after Hatton Cross, and when they reach Terminal 4 they become a train bound for central London which calls at Heathrow Terminals 1,2,3. Trains for Terminal 5 go straight on at Hatton Cross, call at Terminals 1,2,3 and then terminate at Terminal 5 and reverse via reversing sidings to the west of the platforms.

a) Heathrow Terminals 1,2,3
This station was originally a terminus and was called Heathrow Central. It opened on 16 December 1977. It became a through station when the Terminal 4 loop was opened on 12 April 1986 and was renamed to Heathrow Terminals 1,2,3.

b) Heathrow Terminal 4
Opened on 12 April 1986, this station consists of a single platform serving a single track.

c) Heathrow Terminal 5
Opened on 27 March 2008, this station has two platforms, one is a set down only, and the other is a pick up only. Trains terminate here and reverse via the sidings to the west of the platforms.

ACTON TOWN TO UXBRIDGE

Heathrow branch (see page 53)

Ealing Common

After climbing away from Acton Town and passing alongside Ealing Common depot, Ealing Common station is reached. This is the only station west of Acton Town to be served by both District and Piccadilly trains. It was opened by the MDR on 1 July 1879, and was rebuilt by Charles Holden in 1931 to feature a glazed heptagonal ticket hall built from Portland stone. At the east end of the platforms is the west entrance / exit to and from Ealing Common depot. To the west of the station, the line crosses the Great Western Main Line and the Central Line before the District turns left towards Ealing Broadway at Hanger Lane Junction.

North Ealing

Opened by the MDR on 23 June 1903, this station retains a fine example of a District Railway station building, along with many 1903 features on the platforms.

Park Royal

This station was opened on 6 July 1931 ready for the transfer of the line from the District to the Piccadilly. It replaced the former MDR station at Park Royal & Twyford Abbey, a few hundred yards to the north. The station buildings were designed by Welch & Lander, whose work was heavily influenced by Charles Holden. To the north of the station, the Piccadilly crosses over the top of the Central Line close to Hanger Lane.

Alperton

Opened by the MDR in June 1903 as Perivale Alperton, the station was renamed to just Alperton in October 1910. The station was rebuilt by Charles Holden in 1931 and consists of a brick box with concrete lid style ticket hall at street level (the railway is on an embankment here).

A picture taken inside the 'brick box' of Sudbury Town station showing the wall mounted barometer and former news stand, now in use as a coffee bar.

Sudbury Town

Of all the stations designed by Charles Holden, Sudbury Town can be considered to be one of the very finest and features a large brick box with concrete lid ticket hall, concrete footbridge and concrete lamp standards. Internally, the station is relatively untouched and still retains many original features.

Sudbury Hill

Opened on 28 June 1903 by the MDR, the station was rebuilt in 1931 to a Charles Holden design ready for the transfer of the line to the Piccadilly, and is grade II listed.

South Harrow

Although a new station was built in 1935 to a design by Charles Holden, the original District Railway station building still survives and is at the east end of the eastbound platform. To the east of the station are six sidings where some trains stable outside traffic hours. Two rakes (a 3 car and a 6 car) of former Jubilee Line 1983 Stock have been in these sidings since 1999/2000. They are in very poor condition and can be seen from passing trains. Heading west from South Harrow, the line sits atop Roxeth viaduct. Just after leaving the station the stub of the former spur into the South Harrow Gas Works can be seen on the right hand side. This used to receive coal by rail until 1954. The area formerly occupied by the gas works is now a residential area.

Rayners Lane

The line is joined here by the Metropolitan Line's Uxbridge branch from Harrow on the Hill. For a description of the line from here to Uxbridge, please see the Metropolitan section on page 67.

OPERATIONS

Piccadilly Line trains operate to and from a variety of destinations. On the Heathrow branch, most trains are either to Heathrow Terminal 5 via Terminals 1,2,3, or they go to Heathrow Terminal 4 and call at Terminals 1,2,3 on the way back to London. There are also trains scheduled to terminate at Northfields and head back to London via a reversal in Northfields depot. On the Uxbridge line, some trains turn back at Rayners Lane via the centre reversing siding there, with others complementing the Metropolitan Line service through to Uxbridge. Trains can also be turned back at Ruislip via the siding used by engineering trains when leaving Ruislip depot, although this only tends to happen when the service is disrupted.

In the eastbound direction, trains can be reversed at Acton Town, and several trains do reverse here towards the beginning and end of service to get them to and from Northfields depot. Trains usually work through to Cockfosters with some turning short at Arnos Grove. Several trains also start and finish their journeys at Oakwood at the beginning and end of traffic as this is where the west entrance / exit to Cockfosters depot is situated. Two trains also reverse at King's Cross St Pancras at the start of service on a Sunday using the crossover normally used by engineering trains.

Trains on the Piccadilly are manually driven using conventional signalling and train stops.

First trains:

Westbound (Mon-Sat):	0449 Osterley to Heathrow Terminals 4 and 1,2,3
Eastbound (Mon-Sat):	0518 Boston Manor to Cockfosters
Westbound (Sun):	0532 Osterley to Heathrow Terminal 4*
Eastbound (Sun):	0546 Heathrow Terminal 4 to King's Cross St Pancras*

Last trains:

Westbound (Mon-Sat):	2342 Heathrow Terminal 5 to Cockfosters (0114)
Eastbound (Mon-Sat):	2354 Cockfosters to Heathrow Terminals 1,2,3 (0121)
Westbound (Sun):	2300 Cockfosters to Heathrow Terminals 1,2,3 (0026)
Eastbound (Sun):	2325 Heathrow Terminal 5 to Cockfosters (0056)

(From September 2015, Heathrow Terminal 5 to Cockfosters will operate a 24 hour service on Fridays and Saturdays)

*** These two journeys are worked by the same train**

An eastbound train led by driving motor 196 passes through Turnham Green non-stop on 18 May 2014. To the right is a train of D Stock on the District, which will call at all stations along this stretch, with the Piccadilly running non-stop between Acton Town and Hammersmith. A small number of Piccadilly trains do call at Turnham Green at the beginning and end of service.

VICTORIA LINE →

OVERVIEW
Route: Walthamstow Central to Brixton
Type of route / operation: Tube / automatic
First section opened: Walthamstow Central to Highbury & Islington opened by London Transport
on 1 September 1968
Route mileage: 13.3 miles
Number of stations: 16
Trains: 2009 Tube Stock (max of 39 trains required at peak times)
Depot(s): Northumberland Park
Stabling points: Walthamstow / Brixton / Victoria

HISTORY

The Victoria Line was constructed to relieve congestion on other lines in the central area of London. Construction began in 1962 and the first section opened between Walthamstow Central and Highbury & Islington on 1 September 1968. The rest of the line to Victoria was opened in stages, and then on 7 March 1969, the line was officially opened by Her Majesty Queen Elizabeth II. A further extension beyond Victoria to Brixton was opened on 23 July 1971. The line was the first on the Underground to feature automatic operation and has operated this way since opening.

THE ROUTE (WALTHAMSTOW CENTRAL TO BRIXTON)

Walthamstow Central
This station has two platforms on the Victoria (1 and 2). The tracks continue in tunnel a short distance beyond the platforms where there is room to stable two trains outside traffic hours. Interchange is available here with the Network Rail Chingford line and also with several local bus routes.

Blackhorse Road
Interchange is available here with the London Overground Gospel Oak to Barking service. The station seat recesses are decorated with a long black horse in the shape of a road.

Tottenham Hale
The Victoria interchanges with Network Rail here. The tiled seat recesses show a ferry (or 'hale') which used to cross the River Lea nearby.

Seven Sisters
This three platform station is where the line to and from Northumberland Park depot joins the formation. The depot is the only part of the Victoria Line not below ground. Northbound trains for Walthamstow use platform 3, southbound trains use platform 5, and platform 4 is used by terminating trains which detrain the public and then become a service to Northumberland Park depot for staff only. The reversers turn round at the staff platform in the depot before working south again, picking up passengers from platform 5. Trains can also reverse beyond the station on the tracks leading to and from the depot. Interchange with Network Rail is available here.

Finsbury Park
Interchange is available here with Network Rail. There is also cross platform interchange with the Piccadilly, and a physical connection between the two lines. This is used by engineering trains to and from Ruislip depot to access the Victoria Line, and was used in the past to transfer trains to and

from Acton Works for repair (and overhaul until 1986) when the line was operated by trains of 1967 Stock. With the size of the overall bore being greater than that of other lines, the current Victoria Line fleet is built to a slightly larger overall size and cannot leave the line by this connection.

Highbury & Islington

The Victoria Line interchanges here with the Northern City Line from Moorgate and with London Overground services on the East London and North London lines. The former entrance to the Northern City Line is still in place on the opposite side of the road to the current station entrance.

King's Cross St Pancras

This station has a rarely used reversing siding which can be used for turning back trains from central London. This is a large interchange hub which serves the mainline termini of King's Cross and St Pancras and also provides interchange with the Northern (Bank branch), Piccadilly, Metropolitan, Hammersmith & City and Circle lines.

Euston

As well as serving the mainline terminus above, it is also possible to interchange with both the Charing Cross and Bank branches of the Northern Line, the latter having cross platform interchange. Both the Victoria and the Bank branch of the Northern are north to south lines, but they pass through Euston on an east to west axis in opposite directions.

Warren Street

Another interchange with the Northern Line, this time with the Charing Cross branch.

Oxford Circus

Here the Victoria meets the Central and Bakerloo lines and full interchange is available between all three lines.

Green Park

Interchange is available here with the Jubilee Line and the Piccadilly Line (the Victoria and Piccadilly meet three times at Finsbury Park, King's Cross St Pancras and Green Park).

A northbound train of 2009 Stock arrives at Oxford Circus in a rare gap in platform crowds, this being a very busy station in central London. Note the large white apparatus suspended from the ceiling just beyond the dot matrix indicator, this is a chiller unit which pumps out air to cool the platform area. 15 November 2014.

Victoria

The station from which the line took its name. Until the Victoria Line opened, this busy mainline terminus was only served by the sub surface District and Circle lines. There are two reversing sidings south of the station which see limited use, with one train booked to turn here late at night, and another train which stables here.

Pimlico

Not opened until 14 September 1972 (the line through here opened on the 23 July 1971), Pimlico is the only station on the Victoria line that does not interchange with any other railway lines.

Vauxhall

A busy transport hub where interchange is available with local bus routes and the Network Rail station above which is just outside the Waterloo terminus.

Stockwell

Opened with the line on the 23 July 1971, Stockwell offers interchange with the Morden branch of the Northern line.

Brixton

The terminus at Brixton has two platforms with a scissors crossover at the north end. To the south of the platforms, the tunnels continue for a short distance where two trains are usually stabled outside of traffic hours. The Victoria interchanges with Network Rail here.

OPERATIONS

Most services traverse the whole line between Walthamstow Central and Brixton, however, there are some trains which start and finish at Seven Sisters. These run to and from Northumberland Park depot as a service for LU staff only. The Victoria Line has been an automatic railway from its opening, in fact it was the first full scale automatic railway in the world. It began with trains of 1967 Stock which operated by receiving codes from the track, the train operator controlling the doors and pressing two start buttons to start the train. The 1967 Stock was replaced by the current fleet of 2009 Stock in 2011. A new, more modern ATO system manufactured by Westinghouse Rail Systems was also installed, which ran side by side with the old system while the transition from 1967 Stock to 2009 Stock took place. The new system allows trains to run faster and closer together, thus enabling Transport For London to increase the frequency from 27 trains per hour to 33.

First Trains:

Northbound (Mon-Sat):	0526 Brixton to Walthamstow Central
Southbound (Mon-Sat):	0521 Seven Sisters to Brixton
Northbound (Sun):	0652 Brixton to Walthamstow Central
Southbound (Sun):	0654 Seven Sisters to Brixton

Last Trains:

Northbound (Mon-Sat):	0028 Brixton to Walthamstow Central (0102)
Southbound (Mon-Sat):	0053 Walthamstow Central to Seven Sisters (0100)
Northbound (Sun):	2352 Brixton to Walthamstow Central (0024)
Southbound (Sun):	0006 Walthamstow Central to Seven Sisters (0013)

(From September 2015, the entire line will operate a 24 hour service on Fridays and Saturdays)

OVERVIEW

Route: Aldgate to Uxbridge, Watford, Chesham and Amersham
Type of route / operation: Sub surface / manually driven with conventional signalling
First section opened: Baker Street Junction to Farringdon (opened as part of the Paddington Bishop's Road to Farringdon line) by the Metropolitan Railway on 10 January 1863
Route mileage: 41.5 miles
Number of stations: 34
Trains: S Stock (S8) (max of 50 trains required at peak times)
Depot(s): Neasden
Stabling points: Rickmansworth / Uxbridge / Watford

HISTORY

The first part of what is today known as the Metropolitan Line opened on 10 January 1863 as part of the world's first underground railway, between Paddington Bishop's Road and Farringdon Street (now Farringdon). An extension of the line eastwards to Moorgate (then called Moorgate Street) opened in December 1865, followed by further extension to Liverpool Street in July 1875 and to Aldgate in November 1876. This route would later form part of the 'inner circle', but that is where we leave that part of the story (see Circle Line section) and concentrate on the railways which form today's Metropolitan Line.

On 13 April 1868, a single track line was constructed which branched off at Baker Street and went as far as Swiss Cottage. Extension to West Hampstead followed in June 1879, to Willesden Green in November 1879 and to Harrow-on-the-Hill on 2 August 1880. The single line section north of Baker Street was doubled by adding another tunnel in 1882. The Metropolitan Railway had big ideas, saw itself as a mainline railway and pushed itself further and further out from the capital. Pinner was reached in 1885, Rickmansworth in 1887, Chesham in 1889 and Aylesbury in 1892. At Aylesbury, the Metropolitan joined the Aylesbury & Buckingham Railway and operated its trains through to Verney Junction some 50 miles from the centre of London. In 1904, a branch from Harrow-on-the-Hill to Uxbridge opened, followed by a further branch which left the main line north of Moor Park to Watford which opened in 1925. One final branch from Wembley Park to Stanmore was opened in December 1932. The trains to Verney Junction were eventually cut back to Aylesbury in 1936, but with trains coming into London along the Metropolitan from Aylesbury, Chesham, Watford, Uxbridge and Stanmore, the two track section north of Baker Street became a bottleneck. As part of the New Works Programme of 1935-40, new tube tunnels were built between Baker Street and Finchley Road and this new route, together with the Stanmore branch, became a part of the Bakerloo Line from 20 November 1939.

The Metropolitan Railway had started life totally dependent on steam traction, and although electrification was to follow, for many years the electrification ended at Rickmansworth where steam would take over for the final section to Chesham and Aylesbury. The line north of Rickmansworth was eventually electrified, but only as far as Amersham, at which point Metropolitan Line trains were withdrawn north of Amersham, leaving the Metropolitan as we find it today.

Aldgate

Aldgate to Baker Street Junction is described in the Circle Line section (pages 75-77)

Baker Street

The Metropolitan Line part of Baker Street station has four platforms, two centre through platforms and two bay platforms, one either side of the through platforms. At the London end of the through platforms is Baker Street Junction where the Metropolitan joins the Circle and Hammersmith & City lines. There is interchange with these two lines, and also with the Bakerloo and Jubilee tube lines. North of here the line goes into tunnel and, except for a couple of locations where it comes out into daylight, is in tunnel all the way to Finchley Road. Along this stretch there are three disused stations, rendered redundant by St John's Wood and Swiss Cottage stations on the adjacent Bakerloo Line (now part of the Jubilee Line) when that line opened in 1939. The three stations are Lords and Marlborough Road (both closed 19 November 1939) and Swiss Cottage (closed 17 August 1940). Marlborough Road is the only one of the three whose station building still exists at street level.

The disused Swiss Cottage station as viewed from the cab of a northbound train. The platforms can still be clearly seen. A crossover is retained here for use in emergencies.

Finchley Road

At the London end of the station, the Jubilee Line climbs out of tube tunnel to emerge between the northbound and southbound tracks of the Metropolitan. The Jubilee tracks remain between the Met tracks until just north of Wembley Park. There is cross platform interchange between the two lines here. At the country end of the station, Network Rail's Chiltern Line to and from Marylebone comes alongside to make a six track wide railway. Heading north, from left to right, the tracks are: down Chiltern / up Chiltern / northbound Metropolitan / northbound Jubilee / southbound Jubilee / southbound Metropolitan. Beyond Finchley Road, the Metropolitan runs non-stop to Wembley Park, passing through West Hampstead, Kilburn Green, Willesden Green, Dollis Hill and Neasden (see Jubilee Line descriptions on page 20).

Wembley Park

At the London end of the station is a junction giving access to the north end of Neasden depot for both Metropolitan and Jubilee lines There is a physical connection between the Jubilee and the Metropolitan and the Metropolitan increases to four tracks (northbound fast / northbound local / southbound local / southbound fast). The Jubilee Line tracks are still in between the northbound and southbound Met lines and there is cross platform interchange available here for the final time.

Heading north, first of all there is a fan of five sidings. These are used to stable S Stock trains from the Circle and Hammersmith & City lines (they run empty to and from Baker Street). Then the Jubilee Line dives under the southbound Metropolitan tracks and heads towards Stanmore.

Preston Road

This station has an island platform with platform faces only on the northbound and southbound local lines. The station building is situated on Preston Road which crosses over the railway at this point. Some trains run non-stop along this stretch at peak times using the fast lines. Trains also sometimes run fast to help recover the service if there have been earlier delays. Preston Road was first opened on 21 May 1908 to serve the clay pigeon shooting venue of the 1908 Olympic Games. The current station dates from 1931 and is on the opposite side of Preston Road to the original.

Northwick Park

Another island platform only serving the local lines, this time from a subway. This station is close to where the Bakerloo / London Overground and West Coast Main Line pass under the Metropolitan. The station opened as Northwick Park and Kenton on 28 June 1923, being renamed Northwick Park in 1937.

Harrow-on-the-Hill

At the London end of the station the northbound fast connects with the northbound Chiltern and the two share the northbound main north of here. Platform 2 is the southbound Chiltern, but can also be used by LU trains coming in from the north to terminate (the conductor rails end at the south end of the platform). Platforms 3 and 4 are served by northbound Metropolitan Line trains, and platforms 5 and 6 by southbound Metropolitan Line trains. This is the first location since London where interchange is possible between the Metropolitan and the Chiltern Trains Aylesbury service. The station opened as Harrow on 2 August 1880 and was renamed in June 1894.

To the north of the station, the Uxbridge lines dive down and pass underneath the northbound Amersham / Aylesbury / Watford / Chesham lines.

Uxbridge branch (see page 67)

North Harrow

Between Harrow-on-the-Hill and North Harrow there are a set of crossovers between all tracks. North of here the 'main' lines and local lines are paired together, so looking north, from left to right the tracks are northbound Chiltern and Met 'main' / southbound Chiltern and Met 'main' / northbound Met local / southbound Met local. North Harrow station has platform faces only on the local lines. The station opened on 22 March 1915, but the current buildings date from 1930 and were designed by Charles Clark.

Pinner

Opened on 25 May 1885, Pinner acted as the terminus until an extension to Rickmansworth opened on 1 September 1887. There are two platforms serving just the local lines.

Northwood Hills

This station was a later addition to the line, not being opened until November 1933. There are two platforms serving only the local lines.

Northwood

Another station with only platforms on the local lines, Northwood also has a reversing siding to the south of the station for turning trains back from the north. There is also a short stub siding which in recent years has been used for removing withdrawn stock by road for scrapping. The A Stock and the C Stock types left via this siding. The sidings here can also be used to stable engineering vehicles from time to time.

Moor Park

This station has four platforms serving all lines, although except when fast services are running, trains only call at platforms 3 and 4. Chiltern Trains do not call here. The station opened as Sandy Lodge on 9 May 1910, was renamed Moor Park and Sandy Lodge in 1923 and then to Moor Park in 1950. To the north of here is the Watford Triangle where the Watford branch diverges away from the Amersham / Chesham / Aylesbury lines.

Heading north from Moor Park, this is the approach to the Watford Triangle (South Junction). The train is being signalled to the left to join what was the northbound 'main' to bear left towards Rickmansworth. The two right hand tracks go to the right towards Watford.

Watford branch (see page 66)

The Watford triangle does of course have a third side which allows trains to travel from Rickmansworth to Watford. This is mostly used by empty stock workings, but some trains traverse this line in passenger service. At the time of writing, these are the 0515 Chesham to Watford (Mon-Sat), 0608 Rickmansworth to Watford (Mon-Fri), 0700 Rickmansworth to Watford (Sun), 0049 Watford to Rickmansworth (Mon-Fri), 0029 Watford to Rickmansworth (Sun). Please note timetables may change during 2015, please check the timetable link at the back of this book for the latest information.

Rickmansworth

A fan of five sidings to the south of the station, two sidings to the north and number 23 siding beside the northbound line south of the station (which can hold two trains) are used for stabling trains outside traffic hours. The station itself is on a curve and still has a bay platform, which although not used by any service trains, can sometimes see use for stabling engineering vehicles. At the north end of the southbound platform is a water tower that dates back to the days of steam. The station is served by Metropolitan trains and Chiltern trains.

Chorleywood

Opened as Chorley Wood on 8 July 1889, the station was renamed Chorley Wood & Chenies in 1915 and then back to Chorley Wood in 1934. The present name Chorleywood was applied in 1964. At the south end of the northbound platform there is still a Metropolitan Railway signalbox which is no longer used.

Chalfont & Latimer

The junction station for the branch to Chesham. Until the introduction of the S Stock, the Chesham branch was operated by a 4-car A Stock set from a bay platform at the Chesham end of the station. The 8-car S Stock trains are too long to fit in this bay platform, so now all trains to and from Chesham work to and from central London. The bay platform is still in place and is occasionally used for stabling engineering vehicles. The station opened as Chalfont Road, with the name being changed to Chalfont & Latimer in 1915. The station is located in Little Chalfont.

Chesham

The Chesham branch diverges away from the Amersham / Aylesbury line between Chalfont & Latimer and Amersham. It is the only single track line on the sub-surface network, and also the most northerly and westerly points reached by the Underground. The branch meanders its way for four miles up the Chess Valley to the terminus at Chesham. The station here retains much of its charm with a water tower and signalbox still in place and in good condition. The branch actually pre-dates the Amersham line, opening on 8 July 1889 (Amersham was not reached until 1892).

Looking totally out of place on a single track line in a rural location, a train of S Stock led by 21006 heads for Chesham and passes close to Quill Hall Farm on 17 August 2014.

Amersham

Although this is the terminus for Metropolitan Line trains, the line continues beyond here minus the conductor rails and is operated by Chiltern Railways to and from Aylesbury. The boundary between London Underground and Network Rail is north of the station near Mantles Wood. Metropolitan Line trains usually arrive in platform 2 and proceed empty into one of two reversing sidings situated between the up and down Chiltern lines. Once reversed, Met trains usually draw forward into platform 3 ready to work back south. Platform 1 is normally used by Chiltern Railways trains, but can also be used by Metropolitan Line trains.

Moor Park

Croxley

After negotiating the Watford Triangle, the only intermediate station on the branch at Croxley is reached. The terminus was opened as Croxley Green on 2 November 1925 and renamed Croxley on 23 May 1949. The station is actually located in Croxley Green.

Watford

Before reaching the terminus at Watford, the line crosses over the Grand Union Canal on a large steel bridge. The terminus is about one mile from the centre of Watford and as such is one of the lesser used stations on the Underground. Plans are in place and work is underway to divert the Metropolitan via Ascot Road and Watford High Street to Watford Junction, which is closer to the town centre and offers better transport links with London Overground and West Coast Main Line services. This diversion is not expected to be complete during 2015, but the Metropolitan terminus at Watford can be considered to be on borrowed time.

The station itself has a large island platform serving two tracks, plus additional tracks used for stabling trains. The station building was designed by Charles Clark.

A platform scene at Watford Met with a train in platform 1 waiting to depart for Baker Street. The train to the right is stabled in number 21 road. 18 October 2014.

The station frontage at Watford Met taken on the same day as the above photograph. The station building was designed by Charles Clark and dates from the line's opening in 1925.

HARROW-ON-THE-HILL TO UXBRIDGE

Harrow-on-the-Hill

West Harrow

This is the only station served solely by the Metropolitan on the Uxbridge branch (as the Piccadilly Line joins the Metropolitan at the next station). This is a two platform station on an embankment. Although the line through here opened in 1904, West Harrow station did not open until 17 November 1913.

Rayners Lane

At the London end of Rayners Lane station there is a junction where the Metropolitan is joined by the Piccadilly Line and the tracks are shared from here to Uxbridge by the two lines. The station was opened on 26 May 1906 as Rayners Lane Halt and takes its name from the surname of a local farmer of the time. The station buildings date from a rebuild in the 1930s and were designed jointly by Charles Holden and Reginald Uren. At the country end of the station there is a centre reversing siding used by Piccadilly trains, some of which reverse here.

Eastcote

Opened on 26 May 1906 as Eastcote Halt, the station was rebuilt in 1939 to a Charles Holden design.

Ruislip Manor

This station sits on an embankment and is accessed by stairs from the street level ticket hall below. The station opened on 5 August 1912 as Ruislip Manor Halt.

Ruislip

This station was the only intermediate station on the Metropolitan Railway's Harrow to Uxbridge line when it opened on 4 July 1904. The station buildings date from the station's opening. There is also a Metropolitan Railway signalbox at the London end of the Uxbridge bound platform, but this has not signalled a train since the mid 1970s.

To the west of Ruislip station, the line passes beneath Network Rail's Chiltern line and the Central Line close to West Ruislip station. Just beyond that is Ruislip siding, and this is where engineering trains from Ruislip depot gain access to the Metropolitan and Piccadilly lines.

Ickenham

Opened as Ickenham Halt on 25 September 1905. The current station buildings date from 1971.

Hillingdon

This was the last station on the Uxbridge line to open, on 10 December 1923 as Hillingdon (Swakeleys). Although known today on tube maps as Hillingdon, the roundels on the platforms show Hillingdon (Swakeleys). The current station, which dates back to 1992, is not located in the same place as the one which opened in 1923. It is slightly closer to Uxbridge to make room for the A40 Western Avenue which passes beneath the railway on the Ickenham side of the current station.

Uxbridge

On the approach to Uxbridge there is a fan of sidings which are used to stable trains outside traffic hours. Alongside these sidings is a Sainsbury's supermarket which roughly marks the location of the original station in Belmont Road. This closed on 4 December 1938 when the current station in High Street opened. The station has three platforms, the centre track having two platform faces so there are actually four platforms. The station was designed by Charles Holden and is very similar to the terminus at Cockfosters at the opposite end of the Piccadilly Line. Of particular note are the stained glass windows above the circulating area which were designed by Ervin Bossanyi and represent heraldic associations of the area. Also of note are the large clock and 'next train' indicators by the entrance to the platforms.

Arriving in the centre platforms at Uxbridge with the Charles Holden designed concrete train shed dominating the picture. In the distance can be seen the clock and 'next train' indicator and beyond that the stained glass windows.

OPERATIONS

All services on the Metropolitan are operated by 8 car trains of S Stock. At the London end of the route, some terminate at Baker Street while others work through to Aldgate via the north side of the Circle. From London, trains work to either Watford, Chesham, Amersham or Uxbridge. Some are booked to terminate at other locations (such as Rickmansworth and Harrow-on-the-Hill) towards the end of traffic. The Metropolitan has always been known for its fast and semi-fast services that run non-stop between Moor Park and Harrow-on-the-Hill and / or between Harrow-on-the-Hill and Finchley Road. While there are fewer of these nowadays (mostly confined to peak hours), trains can, at times of disruption, run fast to make up time and get back on schedule.

First Trains:

Northbound (Mon-Sat):	0520 Baker Street to Uxbridge
Southbound (Mon-Sat):	0500 Wembley Park to Baker Street
Northbound (Sun):	0655 Wembley Park to Uxbridge
Southbound (Sun):	0635 Uxbridge to Aldgate

Last Trains:

Northbound (Mon-Sat):	0043 Baker Street to Uxbridge (0123)
Southbound (Mon-Sat):	0052 Chesham to Rickmansworth (0109)
Northbound (Sun):	2359 Aldgate to Uxbridge (0100)
Southbound (Sun):	0015 Amersham to Wembley Park (0052)

OVERVIEW

Route: Hammersmith to Barking
Type of route / operation: Sub surface / manually driven with conventional signalling
First section opened: Paddington Bishop's Road to Farringdon opened by the Metropolitan
Railway on 10 January 1863
Route mileage: 16 miles
Number of stations: 29
Trains: S Stock (S7) (max of 33 trains required at peak times - including Circle Line services)
Depot(s): Hammersmith / Neasden (see description of operations)
Stabling points: Hammersmith / Barking / Wembley Park / Upminster

HISTORY

The Hammersmith & City Line operates over the Hammersmith branch, the northern side of the inner circle and along former Metropolitan District Railway tracks to Barking, so it shares its history with these lines. The Hammersmith branch was opened on 13 June 1864 as a joint venture between the Metropolitan Railway and the Great Western Railway. Initially operated by the GWR, a year after opening Metropolitan trains took over services to Hammersmith while GWR trains ran to Addison Road (now Kensington Olympia) via a junction at Latimer Road. The service to Addison Road was suspended in October 1940 due to bomb damage and never resumed.

In 1869 the London & South Western Railway opened a line from Addison Road to Richmond which came alongside the Hammersmith terminus and had its own station called Grove Road. In 1877, some services were projected onto the LSWR's line via a link between the H&C and the LSWR's line just to the north of Hammersmith station. This link was taken out of use in 1916, but traces of it can still be seen north of Hammersmith (H&C) station.

At the east end of what now forms the Hammersmith & City, the Metropolitan Railway had extended beyond Farringdon to Aldgate, and then in 1884, Metropolitan Railway trains were extended via a curve at Aldgate East where trains joined the tracks of the Metropolitan District Railway to St Mary's near Whitechapel. Here they turned off the MDR tracks and joined the East London Railway and worked through to New Cross. From 1936, some trains from Hammersmith were scheduled to run to Barking instead of the ELR. Services from Hammersmith to the ELR were withdrawn from 1939. Until 1990, services between Hammersmith & Barking were shown on the Underground map as part of the Metropolitan Line. From 1990, the line gained its own identity and became the Hammersmith & City Line, denoted by the colour pink on the Underground map. Up until December 2009, the Hammersmith branch had been served exclusively by the Hammersmith & City Line, but from this date, Circle Line services (working Hammersmith-Edgware Road-Aldgate-Victoria-Edgware Road and vice versa) have also served the Hammersmith branch.

THE ROUTE (HAMMERSMITH TO BARKING)

Hammersmith

This is a three platform terminus station situated on the opposite side of Hammersmith Broadway to the station that serves the District and Piccadilly lines. There is no physical connection between the two, but passengers can change between stations at street level with only a very short walk. Recently the buffer stops at the terminus were moved further towards the Broadway in order to accommodate the 7 car S Stock trains which are longer than the 6 car C Stock trains that they replaced on this route.

The current station is not the original that opened with the line in 1864, that was a little further north of here, the current station being opened on 1 December 1868. The station was rebuilt by the GWR in 1907, and even to this day, some of the bench seats bear the initials of the GWR.

At the north end of the station is Hammersmith depot. This is a major stabling point for Hammersmith & City and Circle line trains and can be viewed from the footbridge at the end of the platforms. This footbridge is very lightly used as passengers enter the station at the opposite end and go straight to the next departing train. This footbridge used to extend out westwards to link the station with the Grove Road platforms on the LSWR's Addison Road to Richmond line. There was also a connection from the Hammersmith & City Line into the Grove Road station, and evidence of the former connection, a widening of the track formation, can be seen from departing trains opposite the end of Hammersmith depot.

One of the GWR bench seats at Hammersmith. There are several of these, this particular one being at the Broadway end of platform 1.

Goldhawk Road

The first stop outside of Hammersmith is Goldhawk Road, which opened in April 1914. The railway is on embankment here and remains so to Ladbroke Grove. The station is closest to Queen's Park Rangers' Loftus Road football ground and also serves the south end of Shepherd's Bush market, which the railway looks down upon between here and the next station.

Shepherd's Bush Market

This station opened at the same time as Goldhawk Road, replacing the original Shepherd's Bush H&C station which was situated roughly halfway between here and Goldhawk Road. The BBC TV studios are situated just north of the station here (although the BBC does not have such a presence here anymore), and there is also the large Westfield shopping centre, just in front of which is a large old looking brick building. This was built in 1898 as an electricity generating station for the Central London Railway (now Central Line) and is now used as part of a bus station. The station was called just Shepherd's Bush until 2008, but was renamed Shepherd's Bush Market to avoid confusion with the newly opened Shepherd's Bush station on the West London Line (which interchanges with the Central Line's station of the same name).

Wood Lane

Built in 2008, this station offers easy interchange with the Central Line's White City station which is within walking distance. This station was built without a ticket office, but does have ticket machines. Should any passengers require a ticket office, there is one available just a short walk away at White City (but not for long as ticket offices are due to be phased out). There was a station at Wood Lane from 1908 (closer to Hammersmith than the current one), but this caught fire in 1959 and was not rebuilt. The current station has a roundel from the original Central London Railway Wood Lane station mounted in one of the arches beneath the station.

Latimer Road

At the Hammersmith end of this station, the stub of the former Latimer Road Junction can still be seen. This is where a line branched off to Addison Road (now Kensington Olympia). This line was damaged during an air raid in October 1940 and never re-opened.

Ladbroke Grove

Opened with the line in 1864 as Notting Hill, it was renamed Notting Hill & Ladbroke Grove in 1880 and then to Ladbroke Grove (North Kensington) in 1919. Finally, the current name was applied in 1938. This station is closest to the famous Portobello Market and is also where the elevated A40 'Westway' comes alongside. This parallels the line from here to the next station.

Westbourne Park

At Westbourne Park, the line curves through the station to come alongside the Great Western Main Line in and out of Paddington. Until 1992 there were platforms on the GWML here, but these have been demolished. As trains depart towards London, they run parallel to the GWML, but descend to a lower level. The line then goes underneath the GWML to resurface on the opposite side of the line close to Royal Oak station. This dive under is known as Subway Tunnel and was opened to traffic in 1878. Prior to this, H&C trains crossed the main line on the flat, something that became impractical as traffic levels on both lines increased.

Royal Oak

Situated alongside the throat of the Paddington main line terminus. Today it consists of one island platform serving just the Underground, but it did at one time have platforms on the main line too.

Paddington

Hammersmith branch trains serve platforms 15 and 16, which are situated alongside the main terminus station. There is interchange available with the main line terminus and the Bakerloo Line. It is also possible to change to the District and Circle line station at Praed Street, but it is quite a walk, and remaining on the train until the next stop at Edgware Road gives easy interchange with trains on this line. Leaving Paddington, the line enters cut and cover tunnel, this is the world's oldest underground railway and dates back to 1863. Between Paddington and Edgware Road is Praed Street Junction where the west side of the Circle from High Street Kensington joins for the run into Edgware Road station. There used to be a signalbox in the angle of this junction, and keen observers on trains running between Paddington (H&C) and Edgware Road might be able to make out the former entrance in the wall just before the junction.

Edgware Road

Under normal operating conditions, trains coming off the Hammersmith branch use platform 1, with those heading for the Hammersmith branch using platform 4. The two middle platforms are used for terminating Circle Line trains (platform 2) and terminating District Line trains from Wimbledon (platform 3). Although the two centre platforms are usually used for terminating trains, they are signalled through, so can be used by through trains in either direction.

Edgware Road to Aldgate is described in the Circle Line section (page 75)

Just before reaching Aldgate station is Aldgate North Junction. Hammersmith & City trains turn left here and run via the top of a triangular junction to join the District Line at Aldgate East Junction on the approach to Aldgate East station.

Aldgate East to Barking is described in the District Line section (page 91)

Barking

S7 21387 departs from East Ham with a Hammersmith to Barking service on 3 May 2014. The train actually displays 'Not in Service' as its destination as when it arrives at the next station, Barking, it will terminate and run empty into the sidings. East Ham station forms the backdrop to this picture which also shows the Network Rail line from Fenchurch Street on the left. This part of the line is described in the District Line section.

OPERATIONS

The Hammersmith & City Line operates in conjunction with the Circle Line, both of which use 7 car S Stock trains (S7). Heavy maintenance of these is usually undertaken at Neasden on the Metropolitan Line, while Hammersmith depot undertakes stabling, cleaning and light maintenance.

Trains usually run through from Hammersmith to Barking, but at times of disruption there are a number of places where it is convenient to reverse a train such as at Moorgate and Plaistow. There is a timetabled train booked to reverse at Plaistow towards the end of traffic (listed in the 'Last Trains' section). All trains are manually driven and the line is conventionally signalled with train stops.

First Trains:

Eastbound (Mon-Sat):	0438 Hammersmith to Aldgate
Westbound (Mon-Sat):	0518 Aldgate to Hammersmith
Eastbound (Sun):	0631 Hammersmith to Aldgate
Westbound (Sun):	0641 Barking to Hammersmith

Last Trains:

Eastbound (Mon-Sat):	0011 Hammersmith to Barking (0109)
Westbound (Mon-Sat):	0016 Plaistow to Hammersmith (0107)
Eastbound (Sun):	2336 Hammersmith to Barking (0034)
Westbound (Sun):	0023 Aldgate to Hammersmith (0059)

21349 leads a Barking to Hammersmith service past Farringdon Sidings on 9 August 2014. These sidings were used to stable C Stock, but S Stock trains are too long to fit. The sidings now see little use, although they can still be used by engineer's trains if needed.

OVERVIEW

Route: Hammersmith to Edgware Road, then via Kings Cross, Aldgate, Tower Hill, Victoria, High Street Kensington and Notting Hill Gate to Edgware Road
Type of route / operation: Sub surface / manually driven with conventional signalling
First section opened: Paddington Bishop's Road to Farringdon opened by the Metropolitan Railway on 10 January 1863
Route mileage: 17 miles
Number of stations: 36
Trains: S Stock (S7) (max of 33 trains required at peak times
      - including Hammersmith & City Line services)
Depot(s): Hammersmith / Neasden
Stabling points: Hammersmith / Barking / Edgware Road / Aldgate / Moorgate / Triangle Sidings

HISTORY

The first part of what is now known as the Circle Line opened on 10 January 1863 as the world's first underground railway, between Paddington (Bishop's Road) and Farringdon (then called Farringdon Street). It was built by the Metropolitan Railway in conjunction with the Great Western Railway and the first trains were to the GWR's broad gauge. The 'inner circle' as it was called then was the recommendation of a select committee which wished to see the then new underground lines linked up to connect the London termini of the mainline railway companies. It is worth pointing out at this stage that the mainline railway companies had been prevented from building their railways into the heart of the capital, and were forced to build their termini on the outskirts of the city, thus creating a need for transport between the termini and the heart of the city. After the Metropolitan Railway's first line between Paddington and Farringdon, the Metropolitan District Railway (later to become known as the District Railway) opened a line in 1868 from South Kensington to Westminster. Also in 1868, the MR built a branch off their existing Paddington to Farringdon line from Praed Street Junction (near Paddington) through Bayswater to South Kensington. The MDR built an extension from Westminster to Mansion House which opened on 1 July 1871, and the MR extended eastwards from Farringdon reaching Aldgate in 1876. The 'inner circle' was now almost complete except for a short distance from Aldgate to Mansion House. The similarity in the names of the Metropolitan Railway and the Metropolitan District Railway was no coincidence as it had been the intention that the two companies would eventually merge, however instead they became bitter rivals, with a reluctance to complete the 'inner circle'. It eventually took an Act of Parliament to compel them to do so, and in 1882 the MR extended from Aldgate to Mark Lane (later to become Tower Hill) and the MDR extended eastwards to Whitechapel. On 6 October 1884, a joint station at Mark Lane was opened and the 'inner circle' was complete. That is a very brief description of how the 'inner circle' came into being, but the construction, arguments and operating arrangements of this railway would fill a rather thick book.

More recent history has seen the operation of the Circle Line change from a circle to a shape which more closely resembles a tea cup. Up until 13 December 2009, trains operated either clockwise (outer rail) or counter-clockwise (inner rail) around the inner circle. After that date, and in order to increase train frequencies on the Hammersmith branch, Circle Line trains were extended to Hammersmith. They now operate from Hammersmith to Edgware Road and then run around the Circle on the outer rail via Kings Cross, Aldgate, Tower Hill, Victoria, Gloucester Road, High Street

Kensington and Notting Hill Gate to Edgware Road, where they terminate in one of the centre platforms. The train then reverses and runs round the inner rail back to Edgware Road and down the Hammersmith branch to terminate.

THE ROUTE
(EDGWARE ROAD TO EDGWARE ROAD VIA KING'S CROSS AND VICTORIA)

Hammersmith to Edgware described in Hammersmith & City section (see page 69)

Edgware Road

The current Edgware Road station is much removed from what it was when the Metropolitan Railway first opened through here in 1863. Initially the engine sheds were located here, but were later moved to Neasden due to a lack of space at Edgware Road.

Baker Street

The H&C and Circle lines use platforms 5 and 6 which are set underneath the brick arch roof which dates back to the line's opening in 1863. It is in as near original condition as modern operating requirements will allow. The first trains along here were steam powered, and there are recesses along the length of each platform designed to allow steam to escape. These no longer go out to atmosphere, but have been fitted with lighting to give the impression of daylight filtering into the station. At the east end of the station is Baker Street Junction where the Metropolitan line from Uxbridge, Amersham, Chesham and Watford joins the formation. The Met has its own platforms here set at an angle to the H&C and Circle platforms. The junction is flat, and often eastbound H&C and Circle trains have to wait in platform 5 for a Metropolitan train to clear the junction.

Metropolitan Line (see page 62)

Great Portland Street

Opened as Portland Road in 1863, the station was renamed Great Portland Street in 1917. This is another station that still retains many original features. The building on the Marylebone Road above is a later addition and dates from 1930.

Euston

Opened as Gower Street, this is not one of the better looking stations on this line. Many of the original features remain, but are hidden beneath modern looking tiling. There is no direct link with the nearby Euston mainline terminus, but it is only a short walk between the two.

King's Cross St Pancras

A busy hub serving the two mainline termini at King's Cross and St Pancras, there is also interchange here with the Victoria, Northern (Bank branch) and Piccadilly lines. The current station dates back to 1941 and resembles something more like a tube station.

To the east there is an abandoned station, this being the previous King's Cross station which dates back to 1868. Although it is no longer used, it is clearly visible from passing trains.

Coming alongside the Metropolitan tracks here are two more tracks that are fitted with overhead electrification. These were known as the City Widened Lines and got their name when the Metropolitan Railway increased the size of the cutting here to accommodate two more tracks. They were used by other railways as well as the Metropolitan and linked both the Great Northern Railway and the Midland Railway to the London, Chatham & Dover Railway. Today they are used to carry Thameslink services between the Midland main line and the Southern Region, and the link with the former GNR no longer exists.

The disused station at King's Cross which closed in 1941. Behind the wall to the left is the also disused former King's Cross Thameslink station which closed when the St Pancras International Thameslink station was opened.

Farringdon

Just before Farringdon station, the widened lines dive down beneath the Underground tracks and re-emerge on the opposite side in Farringdon station. There is interchange between the Underground and Thameslink services. The City Widened Lines used to run to Moorgate, and there was a junction at Farringdon where the line towards Blackfriars diverged from the Moorgate line. With the Thameslink platforms extended to accommodate longer trains, the junction at Farringdon was severed and only the line towards Blackfriars remains. The line to Moorgate closed on 20 March 2009. Construction work will see further changes at Farringdon as it will eventually be served by Crossrail. Farringdon (then called Farringdon Street) was the original terminus of the Metropolitan Railway. The station was re-sited to its current position when the extension to Moorgate opened in December 1865 and was also renamed Farringdon & High Holborn in 1926. The station building still bears this name. The station was renamed Farringdon in 1936.

Barbican

Originally called Aldersgate Street when opened on 23 September 1865, there were several name changes before becoming Barbican in 1968. This station used to have a grand overall roof, but it was damaged during an air raid in December 1941. The retaining walls and brackets that once supported this roof are still in situ and clearly visible. There are four platforms here but only two are used. The disused platforms served the former widened lines to Moorgate which closed in 2009.

Moorgate

The abandoned platforms of the widened lines to Moorgate are still in situ at Moorgate. There are also two bay platforms that can be used to reverse eastbound trains back west at times of disruption. The area around Moorgate was heavily redeveloped in the 1960s after wartime bomb damage. The station was rebuilt and the station covered over by buildings.

There is interchange here with Great Northern train services and also with the Northern Line (Bank branch).

Liverpool Street

The next extension by the Metropolitan Railway was to Bishopsgate in 1875. Now known as Liverpool Street, this station once had three platforms, the two through platforms that exist today, and a bay platform used to turn back eastbound trains. This has now been built over, and it is difficult to see where the former bay platform was. Standing proud at the west end of the station is a Metropolitan Railway signalbox which is no longer used but is a listed structure. There is interchange here with the mainline terminus above and also with the Central Line.

The approach to Aldgate station. On the left hand side of the picture, the curve towards Aldgate East used by Hammersmith & City Line trains can be seen turning away. Ahead is Aldgate station with the two Metropolitan Line terminus platforms in the middle and the Circle Line platforms on the outside.

Hammersmith & City to join the District at Aldgate East

Aldgate

On the approach to Aldgate is Aldgate North Junction where the Hammersmith & City Line turns off to join the District Line at Aldgate East. Aldgate station itself consists of four platforms, the two centre ones being the terminus of the Metropolitan Line. The two outer platforms are served only by trains on the Circle Line. A few yards beyond the south end of the platforms is Minories Junction where the District Line joins the 'inner circle'. The south side of the 'inner circle' is shared between the Circle and District lines.

District Line to Upminster (see page 91)

Tower Hill

This station has three platforms, the centre one being a dead end used for terminating trains from the west, usually District services to and from Wimbledon. The current station opened in 1967 and replaced another that was slightly further west and was originally called Mark Lane. There are still some remains of the old Mark Lane station in place. The station serves the Tower of London, but is also only a short walk from the Fenchurch Street main line terminus and Tower Gateway DLR station.

Monument

This station is linked to the nearby Bank station and therefore offers interchange with the Bank branch of the Northern, Central, Waterloo & City and DLR. The station is named after the Monument that commemorates the Great Fire of London in September 1666. It is a stone Doric column which stands within a few metres of the starting point of the fire. This station was opened by the MDR on 6 October 1884.

Cannon Street

This station gives interchange with the mainline terminus above. From January 2015, this station is open daily all day, having previously only opened for limited hours in line with the opening of the mainline station above (the mainline station is also now open daily all day).

Mansion House

One of only two station names which contain all of the vowels, the other being South Ealing on the Piccadilly Line. This was the terminus of the MDR from 3 July 1871 until October 1884 when the line was extended eastwards to Mark Lane. Mansion House has a three track layout which includes a centre dead end platform for reversing trains from the west, although this is currently only used at times of service disruption.

Blackfriars

Interchange is available here with the mainline station above which is served by Thameslink and services to and from the south east. The station has been recently refurbished (2012) and is very modern and bright looking both at platform level and ticket office level.

Temple

The line is very close to the bank of the River Thames between here and Westminster. This station was opened in 1870 as The Temple. The station building at street level is original and is situated on Victoria Embankment.

Embankment

Situated at the country end of Charing Cross mainline terminus, but at a lower level, this station gives interchange with the mainline station above (with a short walk), and the deep level tube lines of the Bakerloo and Northern (Charing Cross branch). It is also handy for the River Boat services that depart from the Embankment Pier on the opposite side of the road.

Westminster

The original terminus of the MDR opened as Westminster Bridge on Christmas Eve 1868. It was substantially modernised in line with the opening of the Jubilee Line through here in 1999, with which there is easy interchange. Heading west, the line now swings away from the bank of the River Thames.

St James's Park

The station entrance is incorporated into the grade II listed Portland stone clad building designed by Charles Holden called 55 Broadway. This is currently the headquarters of London Underground, although LU are expected to vacate the site for new premises in 2015. The building is then expected to be converted into residential use.

Victoria

Until 7 March 1969, the Circle and District were the only Underground lines serving the busy mainline terminus. From that date, the station has also been served by the Victoria Line, with which the sub surface lines interchange, along with the main line terminus and the busy Victoria bus and coach stations.

Westminster station on 15 November 2014. This picture shows an outer rail Circle Line service entering the station worked by an S7 set with 21438 leading.

Sloane Square

This is another station that had an overall roof, and like Barbican, the retaining walls and brackets can still be seen. Towards the west end, a large green pipe crosses over the top of the station. This carries the River Westbourne, a small tributary of the River Thames which starts in Hampstead and flows through Kilburn and Knightsbridge, over the top of Sloane Square station and into the Thames near to Chelsea.

South Kensington

Opened on 24 December 1868 by the Metropolitan Railway and the Metropolitan District Railway. The MR had built a line from Praed Street to connect with the MDR's line from South Kensington to Westminster. Today the station consists of just one island platform, but it used to be much larger with six platforms (inner rail Circle, outer rail Circle, a double sided Circle bay, eastbound District, westbound District and westbound District bay). There are still signs of the former layout along with the retaining walls that used to support an overall roof which has long since been removed. The Piccadilly Line runs directly beneath the Circle and District platforms, and interchange is available between the District and Circle and the Piccadilly.

Gloucester Road

This is where the Circle Line starts to separate from the District. In the westbound (or outer rail) direction, the line splits in two, with District trains taking the left track into platform 1, while Circle trains run into platform 2. Eastbound District and inner rail Circle trains share platform 3. Westbound District can if necessary also use platform 2. A fourth platform, no longer used, displays artwork as part of London Underground's 'Platform for Art' campaign. Interchange is available here with the Piccadilly Line which is in deep level tube below. The surface line platforms were in the open, but the station was rafted over and a shopping mall and apartments built over the top in the 1990s. At the west end of the station is Gloucester Road Junction where the District Line takes the bottom edge of the triangle towards Earl's Court, while the Circle Line diverges towards High Street Kensington.

High Street Kensington

On the south side of this station, the District Line from Earl's Court (the third side of the Triangle) comes in and joins the formation. The two main platforms serve the Circle and District lines while there are two bay platforms for terminating District Line trains. These are currently usually D Stock trains which can terminate at High Street Kensington, but are not permitted in passenger service north of here as they are too long for the platforms (and are not open plan like the S Stock).

Notting Hill Gate

This is one of the finest stations on the Underground with a delightful overall roof which has been sympathetically restored with replica lighting suspended from the roof. Interchange is available here with the Central Line. This station, Bayswater and Paddington (Praed Street) are not long enough to take a full length S Stock. Trains pull up with their front and rear doors beyond the ends of the platforms, with some of the doors in the end cars not opening. As the trains are open plan, passengers can walk through to the nearest available door. Announcements in the areas of the train affected upon departure from the previous station warn of the non-opening doors.

Bayswater

This station still has an overall roof, but it is hard to tell from platform level, apart from a short section at one end. Girders cross just above the height of trains, and above that, the roof is in use as a garage for a car hire company. This line was built in 1868 by the very disruptive cut and cover method, but even at that time environmental considerations had to be taken into account. The most noticeable example of this is between Bayswater and Paddington where the railway passes through Leinster Gardens where there was a row of large houses, a pair of which had to be demolished to make way for the railway. Rather than leave a gaping hole in the terrace, a pair of dummy houses were constructed. They still exist today and from the front look like normal houses, but look closely and it will be noticed that the front door is solid and the windows are painted on. Walking round to the back of the terrace reveals that the dummy houses are nothing more than a 5ft thick wall.

Paddington

Opened with the line in 1868 the station still retains its overall roof. There is interchange here with the mainline terminus and the Bakerloo Line. Paddington is also served by the Circle and Hammersmith & City lines, but it involves quite a walk, and it is considered easier to remain on the train to Edgware Road and change there.

Hammersmith branch (see pages 69-71)

Edgware Road

After departing from Paddington, the Hammersmith branch joins at Praed Street Junction. Arrival at Edgware Road is usually platform 2 for terminating Circle Line trains and platform 3 for terminating District Line trains, although this can be changed for operational reasons.

OPERATIONS

Circle Line trains begin their journey from Hammersmith and traverse the Hammersmith branch through Latimer Road to Paddington and Edgware Road where they join the 'inner circle' and travel via King's Cross, Aldgate, Victoria, Gloucester Road and High Street Kensington to Edgware Road where they terminate. They then perform the same journey in reverse back to Hammersmith. This means that each train calls at Edgware Road twice on each journey, but this reflects the fact that the Circle is a 'hop on, hop off' railway, where passengers using it are making a series of smaller journeys rather than traversing the whole line. It is operated by 7 car S Stock trains which are driven manually using conventional signalling with train stops. There are some stations, namely on the west side of the Circle, where the trains are too long for the platforms and pull up with the outer doors of the train beyond the end of the platforms. The open plan interiors of the S Stock have made this possible with very little alteration to the infrastructure.

23-24 Leinster Gardens showing their painted on windows. This is nothing more than an elaborate 5ft thick wall.

First Trains:

Outer Rail (Mon-Sat):	0448 Hammersmith to Edgware Road via Aldgate
Inner Rail (Mon-Sat):	0527 Edgware Road to Hammersmith via Aldgate
Outer Rail (Sun):	0621 Hammersmith to Edgware Road via Aldgate
Inner Rail (Sun):	0707 Edgware Road to Hammersmith via Aldgate

Last Trains:

Outer Rail (Mon-Sat):	2332 Hammersmith to Edgware Road via Aldgate (0042)
Inner Rail (Mon-Sat):	2350 Edgware Road to Hammersmith via Aldgate (0059)
Outer Rail (Sun):	2311 Hammersmith to Edgware Road via Aldgate (0022)
Inner Rail (Sun):	2330 Edgware Road to Hammersmith via Aldgate (0039)

The first and last trains shown above are the first and last trains that make the full Circle Line trip between Edgware Road and Hammersmith via Aldgate and vice versa. There are a number of shorter trips that finish in locations where trains stable overnight.

Above: *21388 leads a train into High Street Kensington on 18 May 2014. It will be noted that the destination is showing as Gloucester Road. This is quite a unusual for a Circle Line train and was caused by partial closure of the Circle on this day due to engineering works.*

Opposite page: *Pictured shortly after arrival in platform 2 at Edgware Road, a train of S Stock led by 21342 is about to reverse and work a Circle Line service back to Hammersmith (via Aldgate). 18 January 2014*

Notes

DISTRICT LINE →

OVERVIEW

Route: Upminster to Ealing Broadway with branches to Richmond, Wimbledon, Kensington Olympia, High Street Kensington and Edgware Road

Type of route / operation: Sub surface / manually driven with conventional signalling

First section opened: South Kensington to Westminster, opened by the Metropolitan District Railway on 24 September 1868

Route mileage: 40 miles

Number of stations: 60

Trains: D Stock and 7 car S Stock (max 76 trains required at peak times)

Depot(s): Upminster and Ealing Common

Stabling points: Lillie Bridge / Parsons Green / Barking / Triangle Sidings

HISTORY

On 24 December 1868, the Metropolitan District Railway opened its first section of line between South Kensington and Westminster. The Metropolitan Railway had also opened its line from Praed Street Junction to South Kensington on the same day. An extension westwards to West Brompton opened on 12 April 1869. At the east end, the next section to open, on 30 May 1870, was to Blackfriars. This was followed by a further push eastwards to Mansion House on 3 July 1871. At the west end, a branch to Addison Road (now Kensington Olympia) began operation in February 1872 and then another branch reached Hammersmith on 9 September 1874. On 1 June 1877, a short link was opened between the MDR at Hammersmith and the London & South Western Railway, and this allowed MDR trains to reach Richmond. A line was opened on 1 July 1879 which branched off the LSWR's line at Turnham Green and reached Ealing Broadway. The line which had reached West Brompton in 1869 was further extended to Putney Bridge & Fulham (now called Putney Bridge), opening on 1 March 1880. On 1 May 1883, a branch from Mill Hill Park (now Acton Town) to Hounslow Town was opened, followed by a branch from there to Hounslow Barracks in 1884. The line from Mill Hill Park is now operated as part of the Piccadilly's Heathrow branch. Back to the east end of the line, and the MDR opened its extension to Whitechapel on 6 October 1884 and in so doing completed the 'inner circle' with the Metropolitan Railway. The LSWR opened a line from Wimbledon which bridged the River Thames and joined up with the MDR's Putney Bridge & Fulham branch. The MDR had running powers over this line and operated its first train through to Wimbledon on 3 June 1889.

2 June 1902 saw the District (as the MDR had become better known) begin operating to East Ham, following the construction of a link between it and the London, Tilbury & Southend Railway. Some trains also continued along the LT&SR to Upminster. A further extension in the west to South Harrow (then called Roxeth) opened on 28 June 1903. The eventual aim was Uxbridge, and a line was built from South Harrow to Rayners Lane junction where the District joined the tracks of the Metropolitan, over which it obtained running rights to Uxbridge. The first District train ran through to Uxbridge on 1 March 1910.

Widening of the track formation in the east end saw the District's tracks separated from those of the LT&SR and electrification as far as Barking from July 1908. From September 1932, a new pair of electrified tracks were brought into operation to Upminster, which separated District operations from those of the LT&SR (which was now part of the London, Midland & Scottish Railway. Next followed a period of contraction with the Acton Town to South Harrow route transferred to the

84

Piccadilly on 4 July 1932, although the District still operated a shuttle from there to Uxbridge until the Piccadilly took over that too in October 1933. In March 1933, the Piccadilly took over most of the workings on the Hounslow branch, with the District operating in peak hours to Hounslow, an arrangement that ceased in October 1964. This left the District pretty much as we find it today. The history of how the District formed into how it is formed today is quite complicated, and to condense it into an abbreviated form to fit the context of this book is quite difficult, but then it is the longest line with the most stations on the Underground.

THE ROUTE (EALING BROADWAY TO EARL'S COURT)

Ealing Broadway

The terminus of the District Line at Ealing Broadway was opened in 1879. The District takes up just part of a larger station that includes Network Rail (platforms 1 to 4) and the Central Line (platforms 5 and 6). The District has three platforms, number 7 is in the open air, while 8 and 9 terminate under the train shed roof. Of note here are the two 1908 style replica roundels under the train shed. The line climbs away from Ealing Broadway and joins the Piccadilly Line's Uxbridge branch at Hanger Lane Junction and then passes over the top of the Central Line and also the Great Western Main Line.

Ealing Common

This station opened with the Ealing Broadway branch in 1879, but the building dates from a later Charles Holden rebuild of 1931. At the east end of the platforms is an entrance / exit to and from Ealing Common depot, one of two main depots on the District.

Acton Town

The District joins the Piccadilly's Heathrow branch here and there is also another exit from Ealing Common depot on the eastbound District. Acton Town was opened by the District as Mill Hill Park, it was renamed in 1910. At one time there was a short branch to South Acton operated by a single motor car. This used to work out of platform 5, which is still in situ (minus track) but is hidden behind advertising boards. The branch closed in 1959. From Acton Town to Hammersmith, the District calls at all stations, with Piccadilly Line trains running non-stop on this section (with the exception of Turnham Green first thing in the morning and late at night).

Chiswick Park

This station opened in 1879 but was rebuilt to a Charles Holden design in 1931/32. The station building consists of a semi circular station building on which there is a tower complete with roundels. The Piccadilly fast lines pass through the middle of this station and there are only platform faces on the District on the outside.

Richmond branch (see page 88)

Turnham Green

This is the junction station for the Richmond branch, so the District service eastwards from here has a higher frequency of service. The Piccadilly passes through, but does have platform faces against its tracks, and Piccadilly trains call here early morning and late at night.

Stamford Brook

Another station called at only by the District, the eastbound fast does not have a platform face against it, with the westbound Piccadilly and westbound District running either side of an island platform.

An eastbound District Line train of D Stock led by 7129 pulls up at Stamford Brook as a train of 1973 Tube Stock working an eastbound Piccadilly Line service races through. 18 May 2014.

Ravenscourt Park

This station has platform faces against all four tracks. It was opened as Shaftesbury Road on 1 April 1873, being renamed in March 1888. To the east of the station are the remains of the old Studland Road Junction with large chunks of its former embankment cutting between the fast lines and the eastbound local. This is what is left of where the former L&SWR lines from the West London Railway at Addison Road (now Kensington Olympia) used to come in. This was the line that used to call at Hammersmith Grove Road alongside the current Hammersmith & City Line terminus.

Hammersmith

This modern four platform station allows cross-platform interchange between the District and the Piccadilly, and there is interchange with the Hammersmith terminus of the Hammersmith & City and Circle lines via a short walk. Between Hammersmith and Barons Court there is a reversing siding that can be used by trains on either line and from either end. After the next station at Barons Court, the Piccadilly Line dives into tube tunnels, and to ensure that a full size District train cannot be wrongly routed into the tube, there are three glass hoops which are painted on the inside with conductive silver paint, suspended from a gantry over the eastbound Piccadilly. Tube Stock passes beneath this, but if a Surface Stock train passes under it, the glass will be smashed which will throw the signals to danger which in turn will raise the train stops.

Barons Court

This is the last place where cross platform interchange is possible between the District and Piccadilly. The station opened in 1905, although the District tracks were opened through here in 1874. The station building dates from 1905 and has the words 'District Railway' above the entrance.

West Kensington

After losing the Piccadilly in tube tunnel, the first stop is West Kensington. It was originally called Fulham - North End but became West Kensington in 1877. The station is close to Lillie Bridge depot, and a spur turns off the District at the east end of the eastbound platform. This used to be a key location for engineering trains, but sees few of these nowadays. Lillie Bridge is used to stable District trains at night though.

Kensington Olympia

The Olympia branch is usually operated as a shuttle between Olympia and High Street Kensington. At Olympia, the District only uses platform 1 with Network Rail trains using platforms 2 and 3. The District leaves on a single track, which becomes a double track after a few hundred yards. It then joins the Richmond / Ealing Broadway lines close to Lillie Bridge depot.

A train of S stock led by 21378 departs from Olympia with a service for Edgware Road on 18 May 2014. On this day, the Wimbledon branch was closed for engineering works with the Edgware Road to Wimbledon service operating to Olympia instead of Wimbledon.

Wimbledon branch (see page 88)

Earl's Court

This is the hub of the District with the branches from Ealing Broadway, Richmond, Olympia and Wimbledon all converging to head to either High Street Kensington, Edgware Road or Upminster. The station itself has four platforms under a train shed, with platforms 3 and 4 being westbound (with access to all west end branches) and 1 and 2 being eastbound. Trains from the Wimbledon branch can only reach platform 2, while trains from Olympia and the Hammersmith direction can run into either platform 1 or 2. The District opened through here on 12 April 1869, but the first station did not open here until 30 October 1871. The first station was located in the cutting to the east of the current station, but following a fire in 1875, was closed and relocated to its current position. The new station opened on 1 February 1878. The Great Northern Piccadilly & Brompton Railway (Piccadilly Line) reached here in 1906. There is interchange here between the Piccadilly and the District.

High Street Kensington / Edgware Road (see pages 90 and 80)
Upminster branch (see page 91)

Richmond

The District shares Richmond station with Network Rail and London Overground services. Platforms 4 to 7 are suitable for Underground trains and all are terminal platforms. Heading away from Richmond, the District shares tracks with the London Overground North London Line service as far as Gunnersbury.

Kew Gardens

This station was opened on 1 September 1869. The footbridge at the south end of the platforms is of interest as it was built in 1912 with high sides to protect those walking across it from soot and smoke from passing steam trains. The bridge is grade II listed and still has smoke deflectors under the span. North of here, the line crosses over the Thames on Kew Bridge, one of only two places where the Underground goes over the River Thames.

Gunnersbury

This is an island platform and is where, just to the north of the station, District and London Overground services part company at Gunnersbury Junction. The District then passes just in front of the entrance to Chiswick Park station, just after which it joins the line from Ealing Broadway immediately before Turnham Green station.

Ealing Broadway branch (see pages 85 to 86)

Wimbledon

The District uses four bay platforms (1 to 4) and interchange is available here with the adjacent platforms served by Network Rail and also with Tramlink on the far side of the station. There is a physical link between the Underground and Network Rail here.

Wimbledon Park

The District runs along the west side of Wimbledon depot. There is a connection between this depot and the District which is used by main line empty stock workings which travel over the District as far as East Putney Junction where they access the Clapham Junction to Barnes line. The main line trains along here reflect the fact that the LSWR built the line. Ownership was passed to the Southern Railway and then British Railways and the District had running powers over it. In 1994, ownership was passed to London Underground with main line trains keeping their access to the route for empty stock workings. The Southern Railway operated passenger trains along here until 1941. Wimbledon Park station has an island platform served by a station building on the street above.

Southfields

This is the closest station to the Wimbledon Tennis Club and becomes very busy during the Wimbledon Tennis Championships. The platform surface is usually decorated as a tennis court at this time.

East Putney

After passing through East Putney Tunnel, East Putney Junction is reached where the chord to the Clapham Junction to Barnes line goes off. East Putney station has two platforms serving the District, with a third platform against the Clapham Junction bound line which is not used. There are also remains of the old platform on the line from Clapham Junction still visible. North of East Putney, the District runs at roof top height on embankment and eventually reaches the River Thames, which it crosses on Fulham Rail Bridge, which is situated alongside the famous Putney

Bridge. On the east side of the Fulham Rail Bridge, there is a footpath which comes out on the Fulham side close to Putney Bridge station. This is one of only two places where the Underground passes over the Thames, the other being Kew Bridge on the Richmond branch.

Putney Bridge

Opened as the Putney Bridge & Fulham terminus of the MDR in 1880, it became a through station after the Fulham Rail Bridge was opened in 1889. In 1902, the station was renamed Putney Bridge & Hurlingham and in 1932, the station received its current name. The station is not actually in Putney and is named after the nearby road bridge which crosses the River Thames close to here. The station is actually in Fulham with Putney being on the opposite side of the Thames.

Close to the station and very visible from the south end of the platforms is a World War II pill box which was built to defend the bridge over the Thames and still stands proud at the north end of it (see photo on next page).

Fulham Rail Bridge being crossed by a Wimbledon to Edgware Road service worked by a train of S Stock with 21419 leading. Putney forms the backdrop. 25 May 2014.

Parsons Green

Still on embankment, the line reaches Parsons Green where there are a number of sidings used to stable District Line trains outside traffic hours.

Fulham Broadway

Fulham Broadway is alongside Chelsea's Stamford Bridge football ground and is also partly underneath the modern Fulham Broadway shopping centre. This makes the station rather unusual as its south end still has many features intact from when the station was rebuilt in 1905 to cope with Chelsea's match day crowds, but the north end of the station is very modern. When opened, the station was called Walham Green.

A train of D Stock with 7094 at the rear arrives at Putney Bridge station with a Wimbledon to Tower Hill service on 25 May 2014. The World War II pill box can be clearly seen in the right hand side of the picture.

West Brompton
The West London Line comes alongside here and it is possible to interchange between the District and mainline services that call at this station. If the Olympia service is not running, changing from the District to the main line here offers an alternative route to Olympia. This station was the original terminus of the MDR when it opened to here in 1869.

Ealing Broadway / Richmond / Olympia (see pages 85 to 87)

Earl's Court
Although there are discreet modern digital displays on the platforms at Earl's Court, the old destination indicators have been restored and still work with an illuminated arrow pointing to the destination of the next train.

High Street Kensington
District trains for High Street Kensington and Edgware Road take the west side of the triangle junction past Triangle Sidings to emerge at the south end of High Street Kensington station. Some trains reverse in one of two bay platforms (3 and 4), while others continue towards Edgware Road (see Circle Line section page 80).

Towards Upminster (see page 91)

EARL'S COURT TO UPMINSTER

Earl's Court

Departing eastwards from Earl's Court, the line goes through a four track cutting before the line towards High Street Kensington turns off to the left. The line from High Street Kensington burrows underneath and emerges in the cutting on the approach to Earl's Court. District trains take the south edge of the triangle junction to join the Circle Line at Gloucester Road.

**Gloucester Road to Tower Hill (in the opposite direction) is covered in the
Circle Line section (see pages 77-79)**

Tower Hill

To the east of Tower Hill, District trains take the right fork at Minories Junction leaving the Circle Line which curves away through Aldgate to head towards King's Cross.

Aldgate East

Aldgate East Junction is situated at the west end of the station platforms and it is here that the District is joined by the Hammersmith & City Line. The current station opened on 31 October 1938 and replaced the original, which closed to make way for the enlarged Aldgate triangle when it was upgraded as part of the 1935-40 New Works Programme. There is a crossover to the east of the station which can be used to turn back trains, and is used in service by two early trains on Sunday mornings.

Whitechapel

Between Aldgate East and Whitechapel, the line passes through the remains of St Mary's station which closed the day before Aldgate East opened. There are also traces of the former St Mary's junction which used to connect with the East London Line until that became a part of the London Overground network. At Whitechapel, the District (and H&C) emerges into the open on the approach to the station. The London Underground goes over the top of the London Overground here, the line below was a part of the London Underground (East London Line) until December 2007. Interchange is possible between the District, Hammersmith & City and London Overground. The station at Whitechapel is currently a construction site for the Crossrail project. At the east end of the station, the line goes back into tunnel.

Stepney Green

Opened in 1902, this station consists of a ticket office at street level with the platforms situated below in cut and cover tunnel.

Mile End

Still below ground, Mile End station has four platforms with the middle two (2 and 3) being served by District and H&C trains, while on the outside serving platforms 1 and 4 is the Central Line. This is the only place on the Underground where cross platform interchange between a tube train and a sub-surface train is possible below ground. The station was opened in 1902, but Central Line trains did not reach here until December 1946. The name Mile End comes from a milestone nearby which marks one mile from the boundary of the City of London. The road was named Mile End Road, and the station took its name from the road on which it is located. The milestone itself is actually closer to Stepney Green station.

Bow Road

Interchange is available here via a short walk with the nearby Bow Church station on the Docklands Light Railway. This is a most unusual station in that Bow Road passes over the west end of the station, with the east end of the station emerging from underneath on a curve. This means that the west end of the station is in cut and cover tunnel, but the east end is out in the open. A gradient of 1 in 32 takes eastbound trains up towards the former London, Tilbury &

Southend Railway line to and from Fenchurch Street which comes alongside Bow Road and Bromley-by-Bow at Campbell Road Junction and remains alongside all the way to Upminster. Today this line is part of Network Rail and passenger trains are operated by C2C (part of National Express). There was at one time a physical link between the District and the LT&SR here, but there is no longer any connection between the two until Barking.

21396 leads a train of S Stock into Bow Road while working a Hammersmith to Barking service on the Hammersmith & City Line on 29 June 2014. This picture clearly shows how the east end of the station curves out from under Bow Road.

Bromley-by-Bow
After crossing over the top of the DLR's Stratford to Poplar line, Bromley-by-Bow is reached. The station was opened by the LT&SR in 1858, the District reached here in 1902, and the railway became District only in 1962 when British Rail trains ceased to call at the station. The platforms are still in place on the Network Rail lines, but no longer used or cared for.

West Ham
Interchange is available here with C2C services and also with the DLR and Jubilee lines which pass below. To the east of the station is a reversing siding located between the eastbound and westbound lines, and which can be accessed from either end. However, this only sees use at times of service disruption.

Plaistow
Another station that still retains platforms on the Network Rail lines, but which are no longer used or cared for. Plaistow station also has a bay platform which can be used to turn back trains from the west. This is used at times of disruption, but also by one train which is timetabled to reverse here late at night. The station building dates from 1905 and was built at the time the line was electrified.

Upton Park

This is the closest station to the Upton Park ground of West Ham Football Club. The station building which fronts onto Green Street dates from 1904. At platform level, the station canopies still have LT&SR canopy brackets. Disused platforms are still in place against the Network Rail tracks.

East Ham

There are a few things to look out for here. Beneath the canopies, high up on the station wall are signs advertising tea at 2d (two old pence) per cup. The canopies are held up by brackets with the letters LT&SR cast into them, and to the west of the station is a water tower alongside the westbound LU track which was used to water steam locomotives, a truly remarkable survivor. The station dates back to 1858, but the current buildings and platforms served by the District were a later addition and date back to 1905. East of East Ham station is East Ham depot where trains used on the Network Rail lines by C2C are maintained. The LU lines pass right by this depot giving a good view from passing trains.

Barking

Interchange is available here between the District and Hammersmith & City and C2C trains and London Overground's Gospel Oak to Barking service. A connection exists between the Gospel Oak to Barking and the eastbound LU tracks, and this is used by engineering trains coming onto LU from Network Rail. Hammersmith & City line trains terminate here and usually proceed into the sidings to the east of the station to reverse. Westbound District trains approach Barking by diving under the Network Rail lines to and from Shoeburyness, and then cross back over them on a flyover at the west end of the station. The sidings to the east of Barking are used to stable and reverse District and Hammersmith & City line trains.

Although District trains had made it through to Upminster in 1902, this was pre-electrification. After electrification, District trains terminated at Barking and it wasn't until 1932 that the stretch of line east of Barking opened to electric District trains following the quadrupling of this section of line and electrification of the two new tracks. The new pair of tracks and the new stations had all been built by the London, Midland & Scottish Railway (LMS) even though their own trains did not use them. It was done to improve capacity and reduce journey times on their own adjacent tracks. In 1962, the main line tracks were also electrified (overhead wires) and the platform faces against these tracks at stations between Barking and Upminster taken out of use.

Upney

An island platform serving only the tracks of the District. This station was opened by the LMS in 1932, and has only ever had platforms against the District tracks.

Becontree

Originally opened as Gale Street Halt in 1926, the station was rebuilt in 1932 to serve the new tracks served by the District. It was renamed Becontree at this time. All four platforms remained in use until the British Rail trains on the former LT&SR tracks stopped calling at them in 1962. The disused platforms against the former LT&SR tracks are still in place.

Dagenham Heathway

An island platform opened in 1932 by the LMS and served by the District. The station opened as Heathway and was renamed Dagenham Heathway in 1949.

Dagenham East

Opened in 1885 by the LT&SR as Dagenham, the station was rebuilt by the LMS in 1932 to accommodate the two new tracks to be served by District trains. The station was renamed Dagenham East in 1949. There is a bay platform here which can be used to reverse eastbound trains back west at times of service disruption.

Elm Park

The newest station between Barking and Upminster, Elm Park did not open until 1935 and has only ever had platforms on the District tracks.

Hornchurch

Opened in May 1885 by the LT&SR, Hornchurch was rebuilt in 1932 with two new platforms served by District trains. The platforms against the mainline tracks became disused after 1962, but are still in place. There is a crossover at the west end of the station that allows trains to be turned back from either direction at times of service disruption.

Upminster Bridge

The railway here is on an embankment, and this is the only station between Barking and Upminster that is reached by a subway. Inside the station building, there is a reversed Swastika pattern in the floor tiles. This was a common decorative pattern at the time of construction.

Upminster

At the west end of the station, Network Rail's Romford branch joins the formation alongside the tracks of the District. This serves platform 6 at Upminster, with the District serving platforms 3, 4 and 5 and Network Rail's Southend / Shoeburyness line using platforms 1 and 2 and a bay platform numbered 1a. The District tracks carry on beyond the station to reach Upminster depot, one of two main depots on the District and the most easterly point reached by the London Underground.

A train of D Stock led by driving motor 7036 approaches Wimbledon Park with a service for Wimbledon on 26 April 2014.

OPERATIONS

At the start of 2015, the bulk of District Line trains are worked by 6 car trains of D Stock. However, the D Stock will be gradually phased out during 2015 and 2016 and replaced by new S Stock trains. Already, the S Stock is used on the District's Wimbledon to Edgware Road service, which they took over from C Stock during 2014. At the time of writing, work had just been completed to allow S Stock to be used in passenger service at the east end of the District (mostly re-positioning of signalling equipment), and S Stock began passenger service through to Upminster from 16 January 2015.

There are many permutations for trains to operate on the District, with a lot working over the full length between Upminster and Ealing Broadway or Richmond and vice versa. There are then shorter workings between Wimbledon and Edgware Road, Wimbledon and Tower Hill and Olympia and High Street Kensington. The latter service usually only operates at weekends and Bank Holidays or when there is an exhibition on at Olympia. The District has conventional signalling and trains are manually driven.

First Trains:

Eastbound (Mon-Sat):	0451 Ealing Broadway to Upminster
Westbound (Mon-Sat):	0453 Upminster to Richmond
Eastbound (Sun):	0537 Upminster to Aldgate East
Westbound (Sun):	0613 Acton Town to Earl's Court

Last Trains:

Eastbound (Mon-Sat):	0003 Richmond to Upminster (0133)
Westbound (Mon-Sat):	0052 High Street Kensington to Ealing Broadway (0117)
Eastbound (Sun):	2329 Richmond to Upminster (0100)
Westbound (Sun):	2307 Upminster to Ealing Broadway (0038)

Notes

The Trains

The following section describes the trains currently used in passenger service on the London Underground together with stock lists. The following information and abbreviations apply:

DM - Driving motor car (Powered vehicle fitted with a driving cab at one end)

NDM - Non-driving motor car (Powered vehicle with no driving cab)

UNDM - Uncoupling non-driving motor car (Powered vehicle with no driving cab, but fitted with controls at one end to allow uncoupling and shunting)

T - Trailer car (Vehicle with no motors and no cab)

M - Non-driving motor car (Powered vehicle with no driving cab)

MS - Motor shunting car (Powered vehicle fitted with semi permanent couplings allowing trains to be split for maintenance)

Trains have an 'A' end and a 'D' end. Usually, the 'A' end faces north or west except on the Bakerloo where the 'A' cars face south. However, there are some lines that can cause trains to become turned, namely the Kennington loop on the Northern line, the Heathrow Terminal 4 loop on the Piccadilly Line and the Watford triangle on the Metropolitan Line. The common fleet of 7 car trains of S Stock that are used on the Hammersmith & City, Circle and District lines can also become turned depending on what routes they run and where they stable. Although the Hainault loop on the Central Line can cause trains to be turned, the 1992 Stock is designed to be fully reversible and as such they do not have 'A' and 'D' ends.

The lines that are still manually signalled have a form of train protection called train stops. These are positioned alongside signals and consist of a mechanical arm which is raised when the signal is at danger, and lowered when the signal is giving a proceed aspect (see pictures at the base of this page). Trains are fitted with a tripcock, and if a train passes a signal at danger, the tripcock will strike the train stop and make an emergency brake application. If the signal is showing a proceed aspect, the train stop will be lowered and the tripcock will pass over it without making contact. It is not possible to adopt the Network Rail AWS / TPWS systems as these rely on equipment in between the running rails where the centre conductor rail is situated on lines where London Underground trains operate. So where London Underground trains share tracks with Network Rail trains, the London Underground system is adopted. This applies to Gunnersbury to Richmond on the District, Queen's Park to Harrow & Wealdstone on the Bakerloo and Harrow-on-the-Hill to Amersham on the Metropolitan Line. There is also the Wimbledon branch of the District, but main line trains that run empty over this line are not fitted with tripcocks.

Automatic lines (Central/Jubilee/Northern/Victoria) do not have train stops and trains are not fitted with tripcocks.

D78 STOCK

Size of stock: Sub-surface
Year of Manufacture: 1978-1981
Built by: Metro-Cammell, Birmingham
Lines used on: District
Number of cars per train: 6
Train formation: DM-T-UNDM+UNDM-T-DM or DM-T-UNDM+DM-T-DM
or DM-T-DM+UNDM-T-DM or DM-T-DM+DM-T-DM

More commonly known as D Stock, the D78s were first introduced into passenger service in January 1980. They have always been associated with the District Line, and can work all services on the District except for the Wimbledon to Edgware Road route where the short platforms at Notting Hill Gate, Bayswater and Paddington require the use of 7 car S Stock trains with their open plan interiors that allow passengers at the ends of the train to walk through to the nearest open door.

The D Stock run as 6 car trains but are formed of two 3 car units coupled together. Some of these units are double ended with a DM at both ends, and some only have a DM at one end, with a UNDM at the other end. The 6 cars can therefore be coupled together as two single ended units, a single ended unit and a double ended unit or two double ended units. The double ended units can be easily identified as the cab fronts are fitted with inter-car barrier fixings for when they are formed into the middle of a train.

When introduced, the D Stock was considered revolutionary in that it was fitted with Tube Stock size wheels to cut down on the number of standard parts on the Underground. It is also fitted with single leaf passenger doors which have been found to be too small as they slow down loading and

The raised strips fixed to the corners of the cab are part of the inter-car barrier fixings which identify this DM as part of a double ended unit. 7534, Parsons Green, 25 May 2014.

unloading at busy times. The single leaf doors were only ever repeated on the now withdrawn 1983 Tube Stock on the Jubilee Line, but the use of Tube Stock size wheels has been repeated on the D Stock's replacements, the S Stock.

The D Stock is due to be replaced during 2015/16, and the first units were withdrawn on 19 January 2015 (7510-17510-7511 and 7058-17058-8058). Their place is being taken by new trains of S Stock, and once this is completed, the entire sub-surface network (District, Hammersmith & City, Circle and Metropolitan) will be worked by one train type. There are plans for some D Stock to be sold and fitted with diesel engines to work passenger services on some Network Rail lines, but time will tell if these plans come to fruition. London Underground also plans to replace the A stock Rail Adhesion Train with a similar train formed of D Stock.

Working train 062, the 1213 Wimbledon to Barking District Line service, a train of D Stock led by 7101 arrives at Embankment on 10 January 2015.

D Stock
West facing units

DM	T	UNDM	DM	T	UNDM	DM	T	UNDM	DM	T	UNDM
7000	17000	8000	7034	17034	8034	7070	17070	8070	7104	17104	8104
7002	17002	8002	7036	17036	8036	7072	17072	8072	7106	17106	8106
7004	17004	8004	7038	17038	8038	7074	17074	8074	7108	17108	8108
7006	17006	8006	7040	17040	8040	7076	17076	8076	7110	17110	8110
7008	17008	8008	7042	17042	8042	7078	17078	8078	7112	17112	8112
7010	17010	8010	7044	17044	8044	7080	17080	8080	7116	17116	8116
7012	17012	8012	7046	17046	8046	7082	17082	8082	7118	17118	8118
7014	17014	8014	7048	17048	8048	7084	17084	8084	7120	17120	8120
7016	17016	8016	7050	17050	8050	7086	17086	8086	7122	17122	8122
7018	17018	8018	7052	17052	8052	7088	17088	8088	7124	17124	8124
7020	17020	8020	7054	17054	8054	7090	17090	8090	7126	17126	8126
7022	17022	8022	7060	17060	8060	7092	17092	8092			
7024	17024	8024	7062	17062	8062	7094	17094	8094			
7026	17026	8026	7064	17064	8064	7096	17096	8096			
7028	17028	8028	7066	17066	8066	7098	17098	8098			
7030	17030	8030	7068	17068	8068	7100	17100	8100			
7032	17032	8032				7102	17102	8102			

East facing units

UNDM	T	DM	UNDM	T	DM	UNDM	T	DM	UNDM	T	DM
8001	17001	7001	8035	17035	7035	8069	17069	7069	8103	17103	7103
8003	17003	7003	8037	17037	7037	8071	17071	7071	8105	17105	7105
8005	17005	7005	8039	17039	7039	8073	17073	7073	8107	17107	7107
8007	17007	7007	8041	17041	7041	8075	17075	7075	8109	17109	7109
8009	17009	7009	8043	17043	7043	8077	17077	7077	8111	17111	7111
8011	17011	7011	8045	17045	7045	8079	17079	7079	8113	17113	7113
8013	17013	7013	8047	17047	7047	8081	17081	7081	8115	17115	7115
8015	17015	7015	8049	17049	7049	8083	17083	7083	8117	17117	7117
8017	17017	7017	8051	17051	7051	8085	17085	7085	8119	17119	7119
8019	17019	7019	8053	17053	7053	8087	17087	7087	8121	17121	7121
8021	17021	7021	8055	17055	7055	8089	17089	7089	8123	17123	7123
8023	17023	7023	8057	17057	7057	8091	17091	7091	8125	17125	7125
8027	17027	7027	8059	17059	7059	8093	17093	7093	8127	17127	7127
8029	17029	7029	8061	17061	7061	8095	17095	7095			
8031	17031	7031	8063	17063	7063	8097	17097	7097			
8033	17033	7033	8065	17065	7065	8099	17099	7099			
						8101	17101	7101			

Double ended units

DM	T	DM	DM	T	DM	DM	T	DM	DM	T	DM
7500	17500	7501	7514	17514	7515	7526	17526	7527	7538	17538	7539
7502	17502	7503	7516	17516	7517	7528	17528	7529			
7504	17504	7505	7518	17518	7519	7530	17530	7531			
7506	17506	7507	7520	17520	7521	7532	17532	7533			
7508	17508	7509	7522	17522	7523	7534	17534	7535			
7512	17512	7513	7524	17524	7525	7536	17536	7537			

99

S STOCK (S7, S8 AND S7+1)

Size of stock: Sub-surface
Year of Manufacture: 2009 onwards (still under construction)
Built by: Bombardier Transportation, Derby
Lines used on: Metropolitan, Hammersmith & City, Circle and District
Number of cars per train: 7 (S7) or 8 (S8 and S7+1)
Train formation: DM-M-M-MS-MS-M-M-DM (S8 and S7+1)
                        DM-M-M-MS-MS-M-DM (S7)

The S Stock is being introduced across all of the sub surface lines. Already, they have replaced the A Stock on the Metropolitan Line and the C Stock on the Hammersmith & City, Circle and District lines, and during 2015 and 2016, they will replace the D Stock on the District Line. Once the D Stock has been phased out, the entire sub-surface lines will be operated by the new trains.

The trains come in two types, the S8 which consists of 8 cars and is used on the Metropolitan Line, and the S7 which consists of 7 cars and are used on the Circle, Hammersmith & City and District lines. There is a third variant known as the S7+1. These are S7 sets that have had an additional car borrowed from another set to make them up to 8 cars for use on the Metropolitan Line to cover for S8s that have returned to Derby for modifications. There are three sets reformed like this, but as the S8 modifications are reaching their conclusion, it is expected that they will be put back into their proper 7 car formations during the early part of 2015.

An inner rail Circle Line train from Edgware Road to Hammersmith arrives at Paddington (Circle and District lines) with 21407 leading on 25 September 2014.

The internal layout is different between the two types. The S7s are designed for use where the majority of people are making short journeys, and the seating is all longitudinal with more room for standing passengers. The S8s are designed for the Metropolitan Line which is more of an outer suburban railway where passengers make longer journeys, so some transverse seating has been included in these sets to provide more capacity. No alterations have been made to the interiors of S7+1 sets as their use on the Metropolitan Line is only expected to be temporary and they have the same internal layout as the rest of the S7 fleet. All trains have a number of tip-up seats which allow room for wheelchairs and pushchairs. Passenger information displays are sited throughout the train, and these give details of final destination and next station, and also the stopping pattern on the Metropolitan Line (ie: all stations, semi-fast or fast). The displays are also backed up by digital voice announcements.

The S Stock is fitted with air conditioning, the first time that air conditioning has been included on new build trains on the Underground (a car was converted as an experiment as long ago as 1935, but the idea was not taken further). Another innovative feature of these trains is the open plan interior and passengers can walk from one end of the train to the other, which is not possible on any other Underground trains. On all older trains on the Underground, all cars are individual with only emergency access between cars.

The S Stock trains are longer than the trains they have replaced. This has seen an increase in capacity on these lines, and where possible, platforms have been extended to accommodate the new trains. There are some locations where it would have been difficult to extend the platforms, the stations on the west side of the Circle being a prime example where alterations would have been needed to the retaining walls. Here, the S Stock comes to a stand with each end of the train beyond the ends of the platform. The doors only open where they are lined up with the platforms, and passengers in the ends of the train can simply walk through to the nearest door which opens. Localised voice announcements in the areas of the train where the doors will not open are automatically broadcast

Above: The interior of an S7 set showing the continuous saloon and longitudinal seating.

Left: A train of S Stock in the stopping position at Notting Hill Gate with two thirds of the front car beyond the platform end. As can be seen, the position of the retaining walls prevent the platforms being extended.

from when the train leaves the previous station, and a red 'Door Not In Use' sign illuminates above the doors that will not open.

On lines where S Stock operates, marker boards are installed showing where trains need to pull up. The trains do not actually pull up at the board, they are designed so that the driver lines up the stopping position on the board with the edge of the cab window. There are several marker boards which give slightly differing instructions:

An S Stock stopping board at King's Cross St Pancras on the Circle, Hammersmith & City and Metropolitan lines. This board denotes the stopping point for Metropolitan Line 8 car trains, the stopping point for 7 car trains being slightly further back. Note also the sign on the wall for drivers of A Stock, still in place despite these trains having been withdrawn from service in 2012.

S8 - The stopping point for 8 car S Stock trains
S7 - The stopping point for 7 car S Stock trains
SS - The stopping point for both 7 car and 8 car S Stock trains
SR - The stopping point for a train making a reversing move

The S Stock is still being manufactured at Bombardier's Litchurch Lane factory in Derby. Once complete, each train is taken to the test track at Old Dalby in Leicestershire, where a section of line has been fitted with LU conductor rails. They are then delivered to Ruislip Depot directly from Old Dalby. Eventually there will be 191 trains (1,395 cars), making this the biggest single train order in the UK. All movements over Network Rail metals are usually made by two pairs of class 20 diesels (a pair at each end) with barrier vehicles in between the locos and the S Stock. The barriers are there for two reasons, firstly, one end of each barrier vehicle has a wedgelock coupling to attach to the S Stock, while the opposite end has a screw coupling so that the class 20s can attach to, and secondly they are there for brake force, as the S Stock brakes are not compatible with the train air brakes supplied by the class 20s and the S Stock vehicles therefore run unfitted.

The long term plan is for the sub-surface lines to become automatically operated. It is likely that the entire S Stock fleet will have to return to Derby to have the in-cab equipment fitted. These movements are expected to take place throughout 2015.

In the stock list, the S7+1 trains are shown in a separate table, however, they are also shown and highlighted in their proper formations in the S7 fleet, as they are expected to revert to these during 2015.

S Stock, 8-car (S7+1) Metropolitan line

DM (D)	M	M	MS	MS	M	M	DM(A)
21319	22319	25382	24319	24320	25320	22320	21320
21323	22323	25384	24323	24324	25324	22324	21324
21327	22327	25386	24327	24328	25328	22328	21328

S Stock, 8-car (S8) Metropolitan Line

DM (D)	M	M	MS	MS	M	M	DM(A)
21001	22001	23001	24001	24002	25002	22002	21002
21003	22003	23003	24003	24004	25004	22004	21004
21005	22005	23005	24005	24006	25006	22006	21006
21007	22007	23007	24007	24008	25008	22008	21008
21009	22009	23009	24009	24010	25010	22010	21010
21011	22011	23011	24011	24012	25012	22012	21012
21013	22013	23013	24013	24014	25014	22014	21014
21015	22015	23015	24015	24016	25016	22016	21016
21017	22017	23017	24017	24018	25018	22018	21018
21019	22019	23019	24019	24020	25020	22020	21020
21021	22021	23021	24021	24022	25022	22022	21022
21023	22023	23023	24023	24024	25024	22024	21024
21025	22025	23025	24025	24026	25026	22026	21026
21027	22027	23027	24027	24028	25028	22028	21028
21029	22029	23029	24029	24030	25030	22030	21030
21031	22031	23031	24031	24032	25032	22032	21032
21033	22033	23033	24033	24034	25034	22034	21034
21035	22035	23035	24035	24036	25036	22036	21036
21037	22037	23037	24037	24038	25038	22038	21038
21039	22039	23039	24039	24040	25040	22040	21040
21041	22041	23041	24041	24042	25042	22042	21042
21043	22043	23043	24043	24044	25044	22044	21044
21045	22045	23045	24045	24046	25046	22046	21046
21047	22047	23047	24047	24048	25048	22048	21048
21049	22049	23049	24049	24050	25050	22050	21050
21051	22051	23051	24051	24052	25052	22052	21052
21053	22053	23053	24053	24054	25054	22054	21054
21055	22055	23055	24055	24056	25056	22056	21056
21057	22057	23057	24057	24058	25058	22058	21058

DM (D)	M	M	MS	MS	M	M	DM(A)
21059	22059	23059	24059	24060	25060	22060	21060
21061	22061	23061	24061	24062	25062	22062	21062
21063	22063	23063	24063	24064	25064	22064	21064
21065	22065	23065	24065	24066	25066	22066	21066
21067	22067	23067	24067	24068	25068	22068	21068
21069	22069	23069	24069	24070	25070	22070	21070
21071	22071	23071	24071	24072	25072	22072	21072
21073	22073	23073	24073	24074	25074	22074	21074
21075	22075	23075	24075	24076	25076	22076	21076
21077	22077	23077	24077	24078	25078	22078	21078
21079	22079	23079	24079	24080	25080	22080	21080
21081	22081	23081	24081	24082	25082	22082	21082
21083	22083	23083	24083	24084	25084	22084	21084
21085	22085	23085	24085	24086	25086	22086	21086
21087	22087	23087	24087	24088	25088	22088	21088
21089	22089	23089	24089	24090	25090	22090	21090
21091	22091	23091	24091	24092	25092	22092	21092
21093	22093	23093	24093	24094	25094	22094	21094
21095	22095	23095	24095	24096	25096	22096	21096
21097	22097	23097	24097	24098	25098	22098	21098
21099	22099	23099	24099	24100	25100	22100	21100
21101	22101	23101	24101	24102	25102	22102	21102
21103	22103	23103	24103	24104	25104	22104	21104
21105	22105	23105	24105	24106	25106	22106	21106
21107	22107	23107	24107	24108	25108	22108	21108
21109	22109	23109	24109	24110	25110	22110	21110
21111	22111	23111	24111	24112	25112	22112	21112
21113	22113	23113	24113	24114	25114	22114	21114
21115	22115	23115	24115	24116	25116	22116	21116

S Stock, 7-car (S7) Circle, District and Hammersmith & City lines

DM(D)	M	MS	MS	M	M	DM(A)
21301	22301	24301	24302	25302	22302	21302
21303	22303	24303	24304	25304	22304	21304
21305	22305	24305	24306	25306	22306	21306
21307	22307	24307	24308	25308	22308	21308
21309	22309	24309	24310	25310	22310	21310
21311	22311	24311	24312	25312	22312	21312
21313	22313	24313	24314	25314	22314	21314
21315	22315	24315	24316	25316	22316	21316
21317	22317	24317	24318	25318	22318	21318
21319	22319	24319	24320	25320	22320	21320
21311	22311	24311	24312	25312	22312	21312
21313	22313	24313	24314	25314	22314	21314
21315	22315	24315	24316	25316	22316	21316
21317	22317	24317	24318	25318	22318	21318
21319	22319	24319	24320	25320	22320	21320
21321	22321	24321	24322	25322	22322	21322
21323	22323	24323	24324	25324	22324	21324
21325	22325	24325	24326	25326	22326	21326
21327	22327	24327	24328	25328	22328	21328
21329	22329	24329	24330	25330	22330	21330

DM(D)	M	MS	MS	M	M	DM(A)
21331	22331	24331	24332	25332	22332	21332
21333	22333	24333	24334	25334	22334	21334
21335	22335	24335	24336	25336	22336	21336
21337	22337	24337	24338	25338	22338	21338
21339	22339	24339	24340	25340	22340	21340
21341	22341	24341	24342	25342	22342	21342
21343	22343	24343	24344	25344	22344	21344
21345	22345	24345	24346	25346	22346	21346
21347	22347	24347	24348	25348	22348	21348
21349	22349	24349	24350	25350	22350	21350
21351	22351	24351	24352	25352	22352	21352
21353	22353	24353	24354	25354	22354	21354
21355	22355	24355	24356	25356	22356	21356
21357	22357	24357	24358	25358	22358	21358
21359	22359	24359	24360	25360	22360	21360
21361	22361	24361	24362	25362	22362	21362
21363	22363	24363	24364	25364	22364	21364
21365	22365	24365	24366	25366	22366	21366
21367	22367	24367	24368	25368	22368	21368
21369	22369	24369	24370	25370	22370	21370

S Stock, 7-car (S7) Circle, District and Hammersmith & City lines

DM(D)	M	MS	MS	M	M	DM(A)
21371	22371	24371	24372	25372	22372	21372
21373	22373	24373	24374	25374	22374	21374
21375	22375	24375	24376	25376	22376	21376
21377	22377	24377	24378	25378	22378	21378
21379	22379	24379	24380	25380	22380	21380
21381	22381	24381	24382	25382	22382	21382
21383	22383	24383	24384	25384	22384	21384
21385	22385	24385	24386	25386	22386	21386
21387	22387	24387	24388	23388	22388	21388
21389	22389	24389	24390	23390	22390	21390
21391	22391	24391	24392	23392	22392	21392
21393	22393	24393	24394	23394	22394	21394
21395	22395	24395	24396	23396	22396	21396
21397	22397	24397	24398	23398	22398	21398
21399	22399	24399	24400	23400	22400	21400
21401	22401	24401	24402	23402	22402	21402
21403	22403	24403	24404	23404	22404	21404
21405	22405	24405	24406	23406	22406	21406
21407	22407	24407	24408	23408	22408	21408
21409	22409	24409	24410	23410	22410	21410
21411	22411	24411	24412	23412	22412	21412
21413	22413	24413	24414	23414	22414	21414
21415	22415	24415	24416	23416	22416	21416
21417	22417	24417	24418	23418	22418	21418
21419	22419	24419	24420	23420	22420	21420
21421	22421	24421	24422	23422	22422	21422
21423	22423	24423	24424	23424	22424	21424
21425	22425	24425	24426	23426	22426	21426
21427	22427	24427	24428	23428	22428	21428
21429	22429	24429	24430	23430	22430	21430
21431	22431	24431	24432	23432	22432	21432
21433	22433	24433	24434	23434	22434	21434
21435	22435	24435	24436	23436	22436	21436
21437	22437	24437	24438	23438	22438	21438
21439	22439	24439	24440	23440	22440	21440
21441	22441	24441	24442	23442	22442	21442
21443	22443	24443	24444	23444	22444	21444
21445	22445	24445	24446	23446	22446	21446
21447	22447	24447	24448	23448	22448	21448
21449	22449	24449	24450	23450	22450	21450
21451	22451	24451	24452	23452	22452	21452
21453	22453	24453	24454	23454	22454	21454
21455	22455	24455	24456	23456	22456	21456
21457	22457	24457	24458	23458	22458	21458
21459	22459	24459	24460	23460	22460	21460
21461	22461	24461	24462	23462	22462	21462
21463	22463	24463	24464	23464	22464	21464
21465	22465	24465	24466	23466	22466	21466
21467	22467	24467	24468	23468	22468	21468

DM(D)	M	MS	MS	M	M	DM(A)
21469	22469	24469	24470	23470	22470	21470
21471	22471	24471	24472	23472	22472	21472
21473	22473	24473	24474	23474	22474	21474
21475	22475	24475	24476	23476	22476	21476
21477	22477	24477	24478	23478	22478	21478
21479	22479	24479	24480	23480	22480	21480
21481	22481	24481	24482	23482	22482	21482
21483	22483	24483	24484	23484	22484	21484
21485	22485	24485	24486	23486	22486	21486
21487	22487	24487	24488	23488	22488	21488
21489	22489	24489	24490	23490	22490	21490
21491	22491	24491	24492	23492	22492	21492
21493	22493	24493	24494	23494	22494	21494
21495	22495	24495	24496	23496	22496	21496
21497	22497	24497	24498	23498	22498	21498
21499	22499	24499	24500	23500	22500	21500
21501	22501	24501	24502	23502	22502	21502
21503	22503	24503	24504	23504	22504	21504
21505	22505	24505	24506	23506	22506	21506
21507	22507	24507	24508	23508	22508	21508
21509	22509	24509	24510	23510	22510	21510
21511	22511	24511	24512	23512	22512	21512
21513	22513	24513	24514	23514	22514	21514
21515	22515	24515	24516	23516	22516	21516
21517	22517	24517	24518	23518	22518	21518
21519	22519	24519	24520	23520	22520	21520
21521	22521	24521	24522	23522	22522	21522
21523	22523	24523	24524	23524	22524	21524
21525	22525	24525	24526	23526	22526	21526
21527	22527	24527	24528	23528	22528	21528
21529	22529	24529	24530	23530	22530	21530
21531	22531	24531	24532	23532	22532	21532
21533	22533	24533	24534	23534	22534	21534
21535	22535	24535	24536	23536	22536	21536
21537	22537	24537	24538	23538	22538	21538
21539	22539	24539	24540	23540	22540	21540
21541	22541	24541	24542	23542	22542	21542
21543	22543	24543	24544	23544	22544	21544
21545	22545	24545	24546	23546	22546	21546
21547	22547	24547	24548	23548	22548	21548
21549	22549	24549	24550	23550	22550	21550
21551	22551	24551	24552	23552	22552	21552
21553	22553	24553	24554	23554	22554	21554
21555	22555	24555	24556	23556	22556	21556
21557	22557	24557	24558	23558	22558	21558
21559	22559	24559	24560	23560	22560	21560
21561	22561	24561	24562	23562	22562	21562
21563	22563	24563	24564	23564	22564	21564
21565	22565	24565	24566	23566	22566	21566

1972 MKII STOCK

Size of stock: Tube
Year of Manufacture: 1972-1974
Built by: Metro-Cammell, Birmingham
Lines used on: Bakerloo
Number of cars per train: 7
Train formation: DM-T-T-DM+UNDM-T-DM
                  plus one train formed DM-T-T-UNDM+UNDM-T-DM

First introduced on the Northern Line in 1972, the initial batch became known as 1972 MkI Stock, and a later batch intended for eventual use on the Jubilee Line was introduced in 1973. These latter units became known as 1972 MkII Stock. They were built as a crew operated (ie: driver and guard) version of the automatic 1967 Stock cars (now withdrawn) that used to operate on the Victoria Line, and externally, they looked almost identical. Having been used on the Northern and the Jubilee lines, all of the 1972 MkII Stock fleet is now employed on the Bakerloo Line. Mixed in amongst the 1972 MkII cars are a number of 1972 MkI cars that have been incorporated into the fleet and renumbered. Although they appear to be almost identical, look out for black handles on ventilation grilles and internal panelling with a black pattern (instead of brown) in some of the ex MkI cars.

The trains are formed of two units, a 4 car unit at the south end, and a 3 car unit at the north end. The 4 car units have a DM at both ends with the exception of one unit which has a UNDM on the inner end. This has been numbered out of sequence (3299+4299+4399+3399) to highlight to operational staff that it is different.

Since the withdrawal of the C Stock in 2014, the 1972 Stock trains are now the oldest in regular passenger service on the Underground. The plan is that they will eventually be replaced by the 'New Tube for London', but this will be several years in the future.

With DM 3231 leading, train 241, the 1852 Harrow & Wealdstone to Elephant & Castle service arrives at its penultimate stop at Lambeth North. The train number 241 is displayed on the digital display in the cab window. 22 December 2014.

1972 MkII Stock (Bakerloo Line)
4-car 'A' end units (south facing)

DM	T	T	DM	DM	T	T	DM	DM	T	T	DM	DM	T	T	DM
3231	4231	4331	3331	3240	4240	4340	3340	3250	4250	4350	3350	3260	4260	4360	3360
3232	4232	4332	3332	3241	4241	4341	3341	3251	4251	4351	3351	3261	4261	4361	3361
3233	4233	4333	3333	3242	4242	4342	3342	3252	4252	4352	3352	3262	4262	4362	3362
3234	4234	4334	3334	3243	4243	4343	3343	3253	4253	4353	3353	3263	4263	4363	3363
3235	4235	4335	3335	3244	4244	4344	3344	3254	4254	4354	3354	*3264	*4264	*4364	*3364
3236	4236	4336	3336	3245	4245	4345	3345	3255	4255	4355	3355	*3265	*4265	*4365	*3365
3237	4237	4337	3337	3246	4246	4346	3346	3256	4256	4356	3356	*3266	*4266	4366	*3366
3238	4238	4338	3338	3247	4247	4347	3347	3258	4258	4358	3358	*3267	*4267	4367	*3367
3239	4239	4339	3339	3248	4248	4348	3348	3259	4259	4359	3359				

DM	T	T	UNDM
3299	4299	4399	3399

3-car 'D' end (north facing) units

UNDM	T	DM	UNDM	T	DM	UNDM	T	DM	UNDM	T	DM	UNDM	T	DM
3431	4531	3531	3438	4538	3538	3446	4546	3546	3453	4553	3553	3460	4560	3560
3432	4532	3532	3440	4540	3540	3447	4547	3547	3454	4554	3554	3461	4561	3561
3433	4533	3533	3441	4541	3541	3448	4548	3548	3455	4555	3555	3462	4562	3562
3434	4534	3534	3442	4542	3542	3449	4549	3549	3456	4556	3556	3463	4563	3563
3435	4535	3535	3443	4543	3543	3450	4550	3550	3457	4557	3557	*3464	*4564	*3564
3436	4536	3536	3444	4544	3544	3451	4551	3551	3458	4558	3558	*3465	*4565	*3565
3437	4537	3537	3445	4545	3545	3452	4552	3552	3459	4559	3559	*3466	*4566	*3566
												*3467	*4567	*3567

1972 MkI stock cars renumbered

Interior view of middle DM number 3348 showing the longitudinal seating, and also just visible are the transverse seats. Photo taken 10 May 2014.

1973 STOCK

Size of stock: Tube
Year of Manufacture: 1974-1977
Built by: Metro-Cammell, Birmingham
Lines used on: Piccadilly
Number of cars per train: 6
Train formation: DM-T-UNDM+UNDM-T-DM or DM-T-DM+UNDM-T-DM
or DM-T-UNDM+DM-T-DM or DM-T-DM+DM-T-DM

The 1973 Stock was built to coincide with the opening of the Piccadilly Line's Heathrow extension and first entered passenger service in 1975. The passenger accommodation was designed with Heathrow traffic in mind, and all have perch seats near the passenger doors that also double up as luggage space. Each 6 car train is made up of two 3 car units. Most of the fleet is single ended with a UNDM on the inner end, but there are also 21 double ended units that can be paired either with another double ended unit or with a single ended unit. The trains were all refurbished between 1995 and 2000. The plan is that they will be replaced by the 'New Tube for London', but that is expected to be a few years away yet.

1973 Stock (Piccadilly line)
3-car 'A' end units

DM	T	UNDM	DM	T	UNDM	DM	T	UNDM	DM	T	UNDM	DM	T	UNDM	DM	T	UNDM
100	500	300	128	528	328	154	554	354	182	582	382	210	610	410	236	636	436
102	502	302	130	530	330	156	556	356	184	584	384	212	612	412	238	638	438
104	504	304	132	532	332	158	558	358	186	586	386	214	614	414	240	640	440
106	506	306	134	534	334	160	560	360	188	588	388	216	616	416	242	642	442
108	508	308	136	536	336	162	562	362	190	590	390	218	618	418	244	644	444
110	510	310	138	538	338	164	564	364	192	592	392	220	620	420	246	646	446
112	512	312	140	540	340	168	568	368	194	594	394	222	622	422	248	648	448
116	516	316	142	542	342	170	570	370	196	596	396	224	624	424	250	650	450
118	518	318	144	544	344	172	572	372	198	598	398	226	626	426	252	652	452
120	520	320	146	546	346	174	574	374	200	600	400	228	628	428			
122	522	322	148	548	348	176	576	376	202	602	402	230	630	430			
124	524	324	150	550	350	178	578	378	206	606	406	232	632	432			
126	526	326	152	552	352	180	580	380	208	608	408	234	634	434			

1973 Stock (Piccadilly line)
3-car 'D' end units

DM	T	UNDM	DM	T	UNDM	DM	T	UNDM	DM	T	UNDM	DM	T	UNDM	DM	T	UNDM
301	501	101	327	527	127	353	553	153	379	579	179	405	605	205	431	631	231
303	503	103	329	529	129	355	555	155	381	581	181	407	607	207	433	633	233
305	505	105	331	531	131	357	557	157	383	583	183	409	609	209	435	635	235
307	507	107	333	533	133	359	559	159	385	585	185	411	611	211	437	637	237
309	509	109	335	535	135	361	561	161	387	587	187	413	613	213	439	639	239
311	511	111	337	537	137	363	563	163	389	589	189	415	615	215	441	641	241
313	513	113	339	539	139	365	565	165	391	591	191	417	617	217	443	643	243
315	515	115	341	541	141	367	567	167	393	593	193	419	619	219	445	645	245
317	517	117	343	543	143	369	569	169	395	595	195	421	621	221	447	647	247
319	519	119	345	545	145	371	571	171	397	597	197	423	623	223	449	649	249
321	521	121	347	547	147	373	573	173	399	599	199	425	625	225	451	651	251
323	523	123	349	549	149	375	575	175	401	601	201	427	627	227	453	653	253
325	525	125	351	551	151	377	577	177	403	603	203	429	629	229			

Double ended unit 875+674+874 is seen on the rear of train 340, the 2304 Heathrow Terminal 5 to Cockfosters service as it pulls away from a rather wet Barons Court on 15 October 2014.

1973 Stock (Piccadilly line)
3-car double ended units

DM	T	UNDM	DM	T	UNDM	DM	T	UNDM	DM	T	UNDM	DM	T	UNDM	DM	T	UNDM
854	654	855	862	662	863	870	670	871	878	678	879	886	686	887	896	696	897
856	656	857	864	664	865	872	672	873	880	680	881	890	690	891			
858	658	859	866	666	867	874	674	875	882	682	883	892	692	893			
860	660	861	868	668	869	876	676	877	884	684	885	894	694	895			

DM 135 leads an Uxbridge to Cockfosters service into Ruislip Manor on 7 September 2013.

1992 STOCK

Size of stock: Tube
Year of Manufacture: 1991-1994
Built by: ABB Transportation, Derby
Lines used on: Central and Waterloo & City
Number of cars per train: 8 (Central), 4 (Waterloo & City)
Train formation: See explanation below

The 1992 Stock operates across two lines, although cars do not transfer between the two. On the Central Line, they operate as 8 car sets, and on the Waterloo & City Line they operate as 4 car sets. The Central Line sets were built to replace the 1962 Stock trains, and British Rail (Network Southeast) which operated the Waterloo & City Line at the time, tagged five 4 car sets on to the order to replace the ageing class 487 units that dated back to the Southern Railway.

On the Central, each train consists of four 2 car units formed either A+B, B+C or B+D (A = DM / B and C = NDM / D = de-icing NDM). These two car units can then be formed into any of 36 combinations to form 8 car trains, so long as the A cars are at the outer ends. On the Waterloo & City, the trains are formed DM-NDM+NDM-DM.

The Central Line is an automatic railway and the 1992 Stock operates with the Automatic Train Operation (ATO) driving the trains and the Automatic Train Protection (ATP) picking up codes in the track to detect target speeds. They can also operate in coded manual mode, where the train operator drives the train manually but obeys the target speeds being set by ATP. There is also a restricted manual mode where the train is driven manually, with the ATP isolated and the train operator obeying the trackside signals. In this mode, the train is restricted to 11mph.

From 2011, the Central Line trains underwent a refresh with new saloon windows, seat moquette, new lighting in the passenger saloons, and new cab fronts. The new cabs have more red than the originals, giving the front ends a much cleaner, brighter look. One amusing story is the nickname given by staff to the digital voice announcer fitted to all Central Line trains. She is known to crews and maintenance staff as 'Sonia' because she 'gets Sonia nerves'.

91229 is seen on the rear of a westbound service at Bethnal Green on 25 September 2014.

The 1992 Stock on the Waterloo & City Line was ordered by British Rail (Network Southeast) and was originally painted in NSE red, white and blue livery and classified as class 482. When the Waterloo & City was sold to London Underground in 1994, they became part of the London Underground fleet. The Waterloo & City is a self contained railway with no connection to the rest of the Underground. In 2006, the trains were all lifted out by crane and sent to Bombardier at Doncaster for refurbishment, at which point they were also repainted into the standard London Underground livery.

There are five 4 car trains, and unlike their Central Line relatives, they do not operate in automatic mode, but are driven manually on a line fitted with conventional signalling. There are only two destinations on the Waterloo & City, so trains only ever show Bank on one end and Waterloo on the other. Trains are formed into fixed formations DM-NDM+NDM-DM.

2-car B-D de-icing units

NDM	NDM	NDM	NDM	NDM	NDM	NDM	NDM	NDM	NDM	NDM	NDM	NDM	NDM
92402	93402	92412	93412	92422	93422	92432	93432	92442	93442	92452	93452	92462	93462
92404	93404	92414	93414	92424	93424	92434	93434	92444	93444	92454	93454	92464	93464
92406	93406	92416	93416	92426	93426	92436	93436	92446	93446	92456	93456		
92408	93408	92418	93418	92428	93428	92438	93438	92448	93448	92458	93458		
92410	93410	92420	93420	92430	93430	92440	93440	92450	93450	92460	93460		

1992 stock (Waterloo & City Line)

2-car units (facing Bank)

DM	NDM
65501	67501
65503	67503
65505	67505
65507	67507
65509	67509

2-car units (facing Waterloo)

DM	NDM
67502	65502
67504	65504
67506	65506
67508	65508
67510	65510

65508 leads a Waterloo & City Line Bank to Waterloo service into the 'set down only' platform (number 26) at Waterloo on 19 October 2013.

1992 Stock (Central Line)
2-car A-B units

DM(A)	NDM(B)	DM(A)	NDM(B)	DM(A)	NDM(B)	DM(A)	NDM(B)	DM(A)	NDM(B)	DM(A)	NDM(B)	DM(A)	NDM(B)
91001	92001	91057	92057	91113	92113	91169	92169	91225	92225	91281	92281	91337	92337
91003	92003	91059	92059	91115	92115	91171	92171	91227	92227	91283	92283	91339	92339
91005	92005	91061	92061	91117	92117	91173	92173	91229	92229	91285	92285	91341	92341
91007	92007	91063	92063	91119	92119	91175	92175	91231	92231	91287	92287	91343	92343
91009	92009	91065	92065	91121	92121	91177	92177	91233	92233	91289	92289	91345	92345
91011	92011	91067	92067	91123	92123	91179	92179	91235	92235	91291	92291	91347	92347
91013	92013	91069	92069	91125	92125	91181	92181	91237	92237	91293	92293	91349	92349
91015	92015	91071	92071	91127	92127	91183	92183	91239	92239	91295	92295		
91017	92017	91073	92073	91129	92129	91185	92185	91241	92241	91297	92297		
91019	92019	91075	92075	91131	92131	91187	92187	91243	92243	91299	92299		
91021	92021	91077	92077	91133	92133	91189	92189	91245	92245	91301	92301		
91023	92023	91079	92079	91135	92135	91191	92191	91247	92247	91303	92303		
91025	92025	91081	92081	91137	92137	91193	92193	91249	92249	91305	92305		
91027	92027	91083	92083	91139	92139	91195	92195	91251	92251	91307	92307		
91029	92029	91085	92085	91141	92141	91197	92197	91253	92253	91309	92309		
91031	92031	91087	92087	91143	92143	91199	92199	91255	92255	91311	92311		
91033	92033	91089	92089	91145	92145	91201	92201	91257	92257	91313	92313		
91035	92035	91091	92091	91147	92147	91203	92203	91259	92259	91315	92315		
91037	92037	91093	92093	91149	92149	91205	92205	91261	92261	91317	92317		
91039	92039	91095	92095	91151	92151	91207	92207	91263	92263	91319	92319		
91041	92041	91097	92097	91153	92153	91209	92209	91265	92265	91321	92321		
91043	92043	91099	92099	91155	92155	91211	92211	91267	92267	91323	92323		
91045	92045	91101	92101	91157	92157	91213	92213	91269	92269	91325	92325		
91047	92047	91103	92103	91159	92159	91215	92215	91271	92271	91327	92327		
91049	92049	91105	92105	91161	92161	91217	92217	91273	92273	91329	92329		
91051	92051	91107	92107	91163	92163	91219	92219	91275	92275	91331	92331		
91053	92053	91109	92109	91165	92165	91221	92221	91277	92277	91333	92333		
91055	92055	91111	92111	91167	92167	91223	92223	91279	92279	91335	92335		

2-car B-C units

NDM	NDM	NDM	NDM	NDM	NDM	NDM	NDM	NDM	NDM	NDM	NDM	NDM	NDM
92002	93002	92042	93042	92082	93082	92122	93122	92162	93162	92202	93202	92242	93242
92004	93004	92044	93044	92084	93084	92124	93124	92164	93164	92204	93204	92244	93244
92006	93006	92046	93046	92086	93086	92126	93126	92166	93166	92206	93206	92246	93246
92008	93008	92048	93048	92088	93088	92128	93128	92168	93168	92208	93208	92248	93248
92010	93010	92050	93050	92090	93090	92130	93130	92170	93170	92210	93210	92250	93250
92012	93012	92052	93052	92092	93092	92132	93132	92172	93172	92212	93212	92252	93252
92014	93014	92054	93054	92094	93094	92134	93134	92174	93174	92214	93214	92254	93254
92016	93016	92056	93056	92096	93096	92136	93136	92176	93176	92216	93216	92256	93256
92018	93018	92058	93058	92098	93098	92138	93138	92178	93178	92218	93218	92258	93258
92020	93020	92060	93060	92100	93100	92140	93140	92180	93180	92220	93220	92260	93260
92022	93022	92062	93062	92102	93102	92142	93142	92182	93182	92222	93222	92262	93262
92024	93024	92064	93064	92104	93104	92144	93144	92184	93184	92224	93224	92264	93264
92026	93026	92066	93066	92106	93106	92146	93146	92186	93186	92226	93226	92266	93266
92028	93028	92068	93068	92108	93108	92148	93148	92188	93188	92228	93228		
92030	93030	92070	93070	92110	93110	92150	93150	92190	93190	92230	93230		
92032	93032	92072	93072	92112	93112	92152	93152	92192	93192	92232	93232		
92034	93034	92074	93074	92114	93114	92154	93154	92194	93194	92234	93234		
92036	93036	92076	93076	92116	93116	92156	93156	92196	93196	92236	93236		
92038	93038	92078	93078	92118	93118	92158	93158	92198	93198	92238	93238		
92040	93040	92080	93080	92120	93120	92160	93160	92200	93200	92240	93240		

1995 STOCK

Size of stock: Tube
Year of Manufacture: 1996-1999
Built by: Alsthom Transportation, Birmingham
Lines used on: Northern
Number of cars per train: 6
Train formation: DM-T-UNDM+UNDM-T-DM

The 1995 Stock was introduced to the Northern to replace older trains of 1959 Stock and 1972 Stock. They first saw passenger use in June 1998, and by January 2000 they had replaced the older stock. When introduced, they operated with conventional signalling and were driven manually in One Person Only (OPO) mode. The trains they replaced had been crew operated (ie: driver and guard). Since 2014, the entire Northern Line has been operated automatically using the Transmission Based Train Control (TBTC) moving block system.

Although designated 1995 Stock, they were in fact built from 1996 onwards alongside the Jubilee Line's 1996 Stock. They look virtually identical to their Jubilee Line relatives, and were classified as 1995 Stock simply to distinguish them from the 1996 Stock. The 1995 Stock has a more modern traction system than the 1996 Stock, and employs Alsthom's 'Onyx' three phase Insulated Gate Bipolar Transistor system (IGBT). This gives them a different sound to the 1996 Stock which use Gate Turn Off Thyristors (GTOs).

Internally, the 1995 Stock is similar to the 1996 Stock, but where the 1996 Stock uses perch seats, the 1995 Stock has tip-up seats instead. The trains are currently undergoing a refresh with refurbished interiors and cabs. Trains are now also receiving LED destination displays.

A train of 1995 Stock with its D end leading arrives at Hampstead on 18 January 2014.

1995 Stock (Northern Line)
3-car 'D' end units

DM	T	UNDM	DM	T	UNDM	DM	T	UNDM	DM	T	UNDM	DM	T	UNDM
51501	52501	53501	51539	52539	53539	51577	52577	53577	51615	52615	53615	51653	52653	53653
51503	52503	53503	51541	52541	53541	51579	52579	53579	51617	52617	53617	51655	52655	53655
51505	52505	53505	51543	52543	53543	51581	52581	53581	51619	52619	53619	51657	52657	53657
51507	52507	53507	51545	52545	53545	51583	52583	53583	51621	52621	53621	51659	52659	53659
51509	52509	53509	51547	52547	53547	51585	52585	53585	51623	52623	53623	51661	52661	53661
51511	52511	53511	51549	52549	53549	51587	52587	53587	51625	52625	53625	51663	52663	53663
51513	52513	53513	51551	52551	53551	51589	52589	53589	51627	52627	53627	51665	52665	53665
51515	52515	53515	51553	52553	53553	51591	52591	53591	51629	52629	53629	51667	52667	53667
51517	52517	53517	51555	52555	53555	51593	52593	53593	51631	52631	53631	51669	52669	53669
51519	52519	53519	51557	52557	53557	51595	52595	53595	51633	52633	53633	51671	52671	53671
51521	52521	53521	51559	52559	53559	51597	52597	53597	51635	52635	53635	51673	52673	53673
51523	52523	53523	51561	52561	53561	51599	52599	53599	51637	52637	53637	51675	52675	53675
51525	52525	53525	51563	52563	53563	51601	52601	53601	51639	52639	53639	51677	52677	53677
51527	52527	53527	51565	52565	53565	51603	52603	53603	51641	52641	53641	51679	52679	53679
51529	52529	53529	51567	52567	53567	51605	52605	53605	51643	52643	53643	51681	52681	53681
51531	52531	53531	51569	52569	53569	51607	52607	53607	51645	52645	53645	51683	52683	53683
51533	52533	53533	51571	52571	53571	51609	52609	53609	51647	52647	53647	51685	52685	53685
51535	52535	53535	51573	52573	53573	51611	52611	53611	51649	52649	53649			
51537	52537	53537	51575	52575	53575	51613	52613	53613	51651	52651	53651			

3-car 'A' end units

UNDM	T	DM	UNDM	T	DM	UNDM	T	DM	UNDM	T	DM	UNDM	T	DM
53502	52502	51502	53540	52540	51540	53578	52578	51578	53616	52616	51616	53654	52654	51654
53504	52504	51504	53542	52542	51542	53580	52580	51580	53618	52618	51618	53656	52656	51656
53506	52506	51506	53544	52544	51544	53582	52582	51582	53620	52620	51620	53658	52658	51658
53508	52508	51508	53546	52546	51546	53584	52584	51584	53622	52622	51622	53660	52660	51660
53510	52510	51510	53548	52548	51548	53586	52586	51586	53624	52624	51624	53662	52662	51662
53512	52512	51512	53550	52550	51550	53588	52588	51588	53626	52626	51626	53664	52664	51664
53514	52514	51514	53552	52552	51552	53590	52590	51590	53628	52628	51628	53666	52666	51666
53516	52516	51516	53554	52554	51554	53592	52592	51592	53630	52630	51630	53668	52668	51668
53518	52518	51518	53556	52556	51556	53594	52594	51594	53632	52632	51632	53670	52670	51670
53520	52520	51520	53558	52558	51558	53596	52596	51596	53634	52634	51634	53672	52672	51672
53522	52522	51522	53560	52560	51560	53598	52598	51598	53636	52636	51636	53674	52674	51674
53524	52524	51524	53562	52562	51562	53600	52600	51600	53638	52638	51638	53676	52676	51676
53526	52526	51526	53564	52564	51564	53602	52602	51602	53640	52640	51640	53678	52678	51678
53528	52528	51528	53566	52566	51566	53604	52604	51604	53642	52642	51642	53680	52680	51680
53530	52530	51530	53568	52568	51568	53606	52606	51606	53644	52644	51644	53682	52682	51682
53532	52532	51532	53570	52570	51570	53608	52608	51608	53646	52646	51646	53684	52684	51684
53534	52534	51534	53572	52572	51572	53610	52610	51610	53648	52648	51648	53686	52686	51686
53536	52536	51536	53574	52574	51574	53612	52612	51612	53650	52650	51650			
53538	52538	51538	53576	52576	51576	53614	52614	51614	53652	52652	51652			

3-car 'D' end de-icing units

DM	T	UNDM	DM	T	UNDM
51701	52701	53701	51715	52715	53715
51703	52703	53703	51717	52717	53717
51705	52705	53705	51719	52719	53719
51707	52707	53707	51721	52721	53721
51709	52709	53709	51723	52723	53723
51711	52711	53711	51725	52725	53725
51713	52713	53713			

3-car 'A' end de-icing units

UNDM	T	DM	UNDM	T	DM
53702	52702	51702	53716	52716	51716
53704	52704	51704	53718	52718	51718
53706	52706	51706	53720	52720	51720
53708	52708	51708	53722	52722	51722
53710	52710	51710	53724	52724	51724
53712	52712	51712	53726	52726	51726
53714	52714	51714			

1996 STOCK

Size of stock: Tube
Year of Manufacture: 1996-1999
Built by: Alsthom Transportation, Birmingham
Lines used on: Jubilee
Number of cars per train: 7
Train formation: DM-T-UNDM+UNDM-T-T-DM

The 1996 Stock was built to serve the Jubilee Line Extension, and their introduction saw the withdrawal of the relatively new 1983 Stock trains. They entered service between December 1997 and July 2001, and were delivered as 6 car trains. In 2005/6, four 7 car trains were ordered together with an additional trailer car for the remainder of the fleet to bring all trains up to 7 cars. Almost identical in appearance to the 1995 Stock on the Northern Line, the 1996 Stock has a different traction package and uses Gate Turn Off Thyristors (GTOs), similar to those on the class 465 Networker EMUs. This gives the 1996 Stock a distinctive sound which changes tone as the speed increases or decreases, whereas the 1995 Stock has a much more constant and slightly quieter sound.

When first introduced into service, the 1996 Stock was driven manually and the Jubilee Line was conventionally signalled. The line went over to automatic operation using the Transmission Based Train Control 'moving block' system (TBTC). This took place in two stages, Dollis Hill to Stratford and Charing Cross (29 December 2010), and Dollis Hill to Stanmore (26 June 2011). Trains can still be driven manually in 'protected manual' mode.

2015 should see the start of a refresh program for the 1996 Stock, which will include an upgrade of the interiors in a similar style to that given to the Northern Line's 1995 Stock.

96036 is on the rear of a Stanmore to Stratford service as 96120 passes with a Stratford to Stanmore service. Finchley Road, 20 November 2014.

1996 Stock (Jubilee Line)
3-car 'A' end units

DM	T	UNDM	DM	T	UNDM	DM	T	UNDM	DM	T	UNDM	DM	T	UNDM
96002	96202	96402	96028	96228	96428	96054	96254	96454	96080	96880	96480	96106	96906	96506
96004	96204	96404	96030	96230	96430	96056	96256	96456	96082	96882	96482	96108	96908	96508
96006	96206	96406	96032	96232	96432	96058	96258	96458	96084	96884	96484	96110	96910	96510
96008	96208	96408	96034	96234	96434	96060	96260	96460	96086	96886	96486	96112	96912	96512
96010	96210	96410	96036	96236	96436	96062	96262	96462	96088	96888	96488	96114	96914	96514
96012	96212	96412	96038	96238	96438	96064	96264	96464	96090	96890	96490	96116	96916	96516
96014	96214	96414	96040	96240	96440	96066	96266	96466	96092	96892	96492	96118	96918	96518
96016	96216	96416	96042	96242	96442	96068	96268	96468	96094	96894	96494	96120	96320	96520
96018	96218	96418	96044	96244	96444	96070	96270	96470	96096	96896	96496	96122	96322	96522
96020	96220	96420	96046	96246	96446	96072	96272	96472	96098	96898	96498	96124	96324	96524
96022	96222	96422	96048	96248	96448	96074	96274	96474	96100	96900	96500	96126	96326	96526
96024	96224	96424	96050	96250	96450	96076	96276	96476	96102	96902	96502			
96026	96226	96426	96052	96252	96452	96078	96278	96478	96104	96904	96504			

4-car 'D' end units

UNDM	T	T	DM	UNDM	T	T	DM	UNDM	T	T	DM	UNDM	T	T	DM
96401	96601	96201	96001	96433	96633	96233	96033	96465	96665	96265	96065	96497	96697	96297	96097
96403	96603	96203	96003	96435	96635	96235	96035	96467	96667	96267	96067	96499	96699	96299	96099
96405	96605	96205	96005	96437	96637	96237	96037	96469	96669	96269	96069	96501	96701	96301	96101
96407	96607	96207	96007	96439	96639	96239	96039	96471	96671	96271	96071	96503	96703	96303	96103
96409	96609	96209	96009	96441	96641	96241	96041	96473	96673	96273	96073	96505	96705	96305	96105
96411	96611	96211	96011	96443	96643	96243	96043	96475	96675	96275	96075	96507	96707	96307	96107
96413	96613	96213	96013	96445	96645	96245	96045	96477	96677	96277	96077	96509	96709	96309	96109
96415	96615	96215	96015	96447	96647	96247	96047	96479	96679	96279	96079	96511	96711	96311	96111
96417	96617	96217	96017	96449	96649	96249	96049	96481	96681	96281	96081	96513	96713	96313	96113
96419	96619	96219	96019	96451	96651	96251	96051	96483	96683	96283	96083	96515	96715	96315	96115
96421	96621	96221	96021	96453	96653	96253	96053	96485	96685	96285	96085	96517	96717	96317	96117
96423	96623	96223	96023	96455	96655	96255	96055	96487	96687	96287	96087	96519	96719	96319	96119
96425	96625	96225	96025	96457	96657	96257	96057	96489	96689	96289	96089	96521	96721	96321	96121
96427	96627	96227	96027	96459	96659	96259	96059	96491	96691	96291	96091	96523	96723	96323	96123
96429	96629	96229	96029	96461	96661	96261	96061	96493	96693	96293	96093	96525	96725	96325	96125
96431	96631	96231	96031	96463	96663	96263	96063	96495	96695	96295	96095				

Notes

2009 STOCK

Size of stock: Tube
Year of Manufacture: 2006-2011
Built by: Bombardier Transportation, Derby
Lines used on: Victoria
Number of cars per train: 8
Train formation: DM-T-NDM-UNDM+UNDM-NDM-T-DM

The 2009 Stock was built to replace the 1967 Stock which had worked the Victoria Line since its opening. The trains have been designed solely for use on the Victoria, although they belong to the same 'family' as the sub-surface S Stock. They operate automatically using the Westinghouse 'distance to go' ATO/ATP system, a system which had to be installed and operated alongside the existing ATO system on the Victoria to allow the 2009 Stock and 1967 Stock to operate side by side during the period of changeover.

A pre-production train underwent testing on the Victoria Line from May 2007 onwards, with a second pre-production train going into passenger service in July 2009. The production trains were then brought into service, with the 1967 Stock finally working their last services on 30th June 2011.

When the Victoria Line was constructed, the size of the overall bore of the tunnels was slightly larger than on other lines. This has allowed the 2009 Stock to be built 40mm wider than the 1967 Stock, and with a slimmer body shell and externally hung doors, there is more room inside the train. The downside to this though, is that the trains cannot leave the Victoria Line except by road. The Victoria is connected to the rest of the Underground via a connection with the Piccadilly at Finsbury Park, but the trains are too large for the Piccadilly Line tunnels.

Internally, the trains are well equipped for carrying passengers with impaired mobility, with tip up seats that create space for wheelchairs and pushchairs, and the grab poles in the doorways are offset to allow the passage of a wheelchair. There is also lighting at floor level by each door which illuminates when the doors are open to assist anybody with visual impairment.

2009 Stock (Victoria line)
8-car units

DM(A)	T	NDM	UNDM	UNDM	NDM	T	DM(D)	DM(A)	T	NDM	UNDM	UNDM	NDM	T	DM(D)
11001	12001	13001	14001	14002	13002	12002	11002	11049	12049	13049	14049	14050	13050	12050	11050
11003	12003	13003	14003	14004	13004	12004	11004	11051	12051	13051	14051	14052	13052	12052	11052
11005	12005	13005	14005	14006	13006	12006	11006	11053	12053	13053	14053	14054	13054	12054	11054
11007	12007	13007	14007	14008	13008	12008	11008	11055	12055	13055	14055	14056	13056	12056	11056
11009	12009	13009	14009	14010	13010	12010	11010	11057	12057	13057	14057	14058	13058	12058	11058
11011	12011	13011	14011	14012	13012	12012	11012	11059	12059	13059	14059	14060	13060	12060	11060
11013	12013	13013	14013	14014	13014	12014	11014	11061	12061	13061	14061	14062	13062	12062	11062
11015	12015	13015	14015	14016	13016	12016	11016	11063	12063	13063	14063	14064	13064	12064	11064
11017	12017	13017	14017	14018	13018	12018	11018	11065	12065	13065	14065	14066	13066	12066	11066
11019	12019	13019	14019	14020	13020	12020	11020	11067	12067	13067	14067	14068	13068	12068	11068
11021	12021	13021	14021	14022	13022	12022	11022	11069	12069	13069	14069	14070	13070	12070	11070
11023	12023	13023	14023	14024	13024	12024	11024	11071	12071	13071	14071	14072	13072	12072	11072
11025	12025	13025	14025	14026	13026	12026	11026	11073	12073	13073	14073	14074	13074	12074	11074
11027	12027	13027	14027	14028	13028	12028	11028	11075	12075	13075	14075	14076	13076	12076	11076
11029	12029	13029	14029	14030	13030	12030	11030	11077	12077	13077	14077	14078	13078	12078	11078
11031	12031	13031	14031	14032	13032	12032	11032	11079	12079	13079	14079	14080	13080	12080	11080
11033	12033	13033	14033	14034	13034	12034	11034	11081	12081	13081	14081	14082	13082	12082	11082
11035	12035	13035	14035	14036	13036	12036	11036	11083	12083	13083	14083	14084	13084	12084	11084
11037	12037	13037	14037	14038	13038	12038	11038	11085	12085	13085	14085	14086	13086	12086	11086
11039	12039	13039	14039	14040	13040	12040	11040	11087	12087	13087	14087	14088	13088	12088	11088
11041	12041	13041	14041	14042	13042	12042	11042	11089	12089	13089	14089	14090	13090	12090	11090
11043	12043	13043	14043	14044	13044	12044	11044	11091	12091	13091	14091	14092	13092	12092	11092
11045	12045	13045	14045	14046	13046	12046	11046	11093	12093	13093	14093	14094	13094	12094	11094
11047	12047	13047	14047	14048	13048	12048	11048								

Notes

Opposite page: Arriving at Pimlico is a southbound Victoria Line train headed by 11045 on 15 November 2014. Noticeable under the number is a poppy sticker. Many LU trains are adorned with these in the autumn as a mark of respect for Remembrance Day.

ENGINEERING TRAINS

Each night, the London Underground shuts down for a period of around 4 hours. Even when the Underground commences 24 hour operation in autumn 2015, this will only apply to Friday and Saturday nights on selected lines, with the remaining nights of the week still available to the engineers. This is the best time to access the system to carry out maintenance and repairs, and also to patrol sections of line to ensure that all is in good order. It is also the time when adverts in stations are changed and stretches of tunnel are cleaned of the dirt that builds up over time in the tunnels, and which can become a fire hazard if not kept in check (mostly human hair, clothing fibres, litter etc...). Some jobs can be carried out by a 'team in a van' turning up at a location and carrying out a specific task, but some jobs require the movement of heavy machinery and materials by rail to the worksite. For this purpose, a fleet of engineering vehicles are used for a variety of tasks around the system. Some are purpose built for their tasks while others are converted from old passenger stock. The fleet consists of locomotives, wagons, cranes, rail adhesion trains, a track recording train, an asset inspection train along with various rail grinders and rail millers. It is rare to see engineering trains during daylight as they spend most of their time hidden away and come out at the end of traffic hours and go back into hiding at the start of traffic the next day. There is a Track Recording Train which often runs during the day, but you either have to know when and where it is running or be very lucky to see it. The Rail Adhesion Trains are a little more predictable, being used regularly over selected routes during the autumn to combat leaf fall.

In addition to the overnight maintenance, there are also bigger engineering tasks undertaken over longer periods, usually weekends, where sections of lines are closed (often with rail replacement buses carrying passengers) while track replacement, drainage work, signalling and other major tasks are undertaken. These often involve London Underground's own fleet of engineering vehicles, but on the sub-surface network can also involve trains that come in from Network Rail. While inconvenient for the traveller, these shut downs are aimed at improving the Underground network and represent a substantial investment in the infrastructure. Details of engineering work can usually be found in advance on the Transport For London website.

The engineering fleet is maintained by the 'Transplant' arm of London Underground.

Lillie Bridge Depot

Situated next to Earl's Court, this is where track sections, buffer stops, bridge decking etc is manufactured. With the forthcoming redevelopment of Earl's Court, London Underground plans to move the Lillie Bridge operation to Ruislip by 2016.

Ruislip Depot

Besides being one of the main depots on the Central Line, Ruislip is also home to most of the engineering fleet. Engineering trains going out on overnight jobs and weekend possessions usually come from here. Materials such as ballast, sleepers and rail are brought in by rail using the connection between the depot and Network Rail.

Battery Locomotives

Transplant has a fleet of 29 battery locomotives from three batches. The oldest are L20 to L32 which were built by Metro-Cammell in 1964/1965, and the oldest, L20, celebrated its 50th birthday in late 2014, being delivered to Ruislip depot on 8 December 1964. The next batch of locos are numbered L15 to L19 and were also built by Metro-Cammell, in 1970. Finally, there are L44 to L54 which were built in 1973/1974 by the Doncaster Works of British Rail Engineering Ltd (BREL). All are very similar in design and are to tube gauge. Technically, the locos are battery-electric locomotives, as they can either draw traction power from the 630V conductor rails like any other Underground train, or they can take their power from 320V on-board batteries. They are used to haul engineering trains around the Underground network, and they usually run on electric power until they reach the worksite, where the traction current will usually be turned off, and they will make any movements required using power from their batteries.

All of the fleet is fitted with tripcocks for use on conventionally signalled lines, but several are also fitted with the Central Line ATP and / or the TBTC signalling system as used on the Jubilee and Northern lines. Like most other Underground trains, battery locos have an 'A' end and a 'D' end. Four of the BREL locomotives (L50-L53) have had their buffers and screw / buckeye couplings removed at the 'A' end for use with long welded rail trains. They can also be used on other engineering trains, but always have the 'D' end coupled to the wagons. Trains are usually top and tailed with a battery loco on each end. This cuts down the time taken to reverse while en route to site, but also assists at the work site itself where the train may need to be split to access the materials and equipment being carried.

The fleet is currently undergoing life extension modifications, involving new batteries and revised cab layouts with the side doors removed. This makes the space in the cab larger, but the crew have to enter and exit the loco through the door in the cab front. This has necessitated the fitting of safety railings to the ends of the locos. At the time of writing, just under half of the fleet had received the modifications.

One of the modified battery locos, L24, passes through Rayners Lane on 20 November 2014 with train 635, a 2301 Ruislip depot to Becontree ballast train formed of hopper wagons. This section of line can often be quite busy with engineering trains at the start and end of traffic.

Schöma Diesel Locomotives

In 2000, Transplant inherited a fleet of 14 diesel locomotives that had been used during the construction of the Jubilee Line Extension. These locomotives were built by Schöma in 1995 to type CFL-500VR. They have a 500hp diesel engine and are fitted with exhaust scrubbers so that emissions are kept to a minimum, which allows them to be used in sub-surface tunnels (but not usually in tube tunnels). They share some duties with battery locos, but also see use at Lillie Bridge and Ruislip as shunters. The Schöma fleet is to be converted into battery locomotives and will operate in pairs to supplement the current battery loco fleet. This work is being undertaken by Clayton's in Burton-on-Trent, and the first two, L2 and L5, are expected to be completed early in 2015. L4 and L8 are also at Clayton's for conversion.

Track Recording Train

This train consists of two 1960 Tube Stock driving motors with a 1973 Stock trailer sandwiched between them. It was formed in 1987 and is used to monitor track condition throughout the Underground. The recording equipment is located in the 1973 Stock trailer. The train is fitted with

Above: L54 passes Harrow-on-the-Hill with train 545, the 2251 Ruislip Depot to Temple on 31 October 2014.

Below: Schöma diesel locos L12 and L3 are seen at Ongar during a visit to the Epping & Ongar Railway on 27 September 2014.

tripcocks for use on conventionally signalled lines, and with the Central Line's ATP system. It can also be used to record on the Jubilee, Northern and Victoria lines outside of normal traffic hours. The Track Recording Train is due to be replaced by the Asset Inspection Train, and is likely to be withdrawn during 2015.

Asset Inspection Train
Formed of 1972 MkI Stock and 1967 Stock cars, this 6 car train is set to replace the Track Recording Train for monitoring track and other lineside assets. At the time of writing, it had yet to enter service, but had made several test runs. Eventually, it is planned that it will be compatible with the signalling on all lines, but does not yet have all of the systems fitted.

Rail Adhesion Trains
The autumn leaf fall season causes problems for parts of the Metropolitan and Central lines. For this reason, there are three 'Rail Adhesion Trains' (often referred to as 'RATs'), which apply a sticky paste called 'Sandite' to the railhead to assist with adhesion when rail conditions are compromised due to leaves on the line. The two Central Line trains are formed of 1962 Stock cars (with one 1959 Stock car). One train is formed of 5 cars, and deals with the west end of the Central Line between West Ruislip and White City including the Ealing Broadway branch, while the other train is formed of 8 cars and deals with the east end of the Central between Newbury Park and Woodford and between Epping and Leytonstone. On the Metropolitan Line, a 4 car train of A Stock has an additional car (Rail Adhesion Car 6036) inserted into its formation and is used between Neasden depot and Amersham including Watford, Chesham and Uxbridge. All of the above trains are used between the end of September and December and run to regular patterns as railhead conditions dictate. The 5 car Central Line RAT can also be used for towing other Tube Stock, and is sometimes reduced to 4 cars for this role.

Track Maintenance Machines
Transplant has three tube gauged tamping machines (TMM771-773) built in 1980 by Plasser & Theurer, and one full size points and crossings tamping machine (TMM774). There is also a fifth machine (not to tube gauge) on hire from Schweerbau which may pass into Transplant ownership.

These vehicles are capable of self propulsion. For locations that can be reached without passing through tube tunnels, they often run to site under their own power, but where transit through tube tunnels is required, they are usually hauled to site by battery locomotives.

Rail Grinders and Rail Millers

Various rail grinders and rail millers can be found in use on the Underground to maintain the integrity of the railhead. These are owned by contractors Schweerbau, Strabag and Speno, and are not part of Transplant stock.

Tunnel Cleaning Train

A new tunnel cleaning train was to be formed using four 1967 Stock DMs (two at each end) as traction. This project has been cancelled, but the 1967 Stock DMs may find another use and are currently stored at Acton Works.

Non-Powered Vehicles

There is a large fleet of wagons used for various purposes. These include ballast hoppers, general purpose wagons, spoil and ballast wagons, drum wagons, well wagons and cranes. Some have been adapted for specific roles, while others are for general use.

General Purpose wagon GP935 is seen formed into an engineer's train with a load of fresh ballast passing through Notting Hill Gate on 24 February 2013. The GP wagons can be used to carry a variety of materials including fresh ballast, spoil and various plant and materials.

Increase Your Chances of Seeing Engineering Trains

Engineering trains, and the battery locomotives in particular, are of interest to a lot of London Underground enthusiasts. They spend a lot of their time hiding away and come out at night when the Underground is closed. Even when they are on weekend long engineering jobs, they can be difficult to find, and unless you are lucky and manage to find one parked near a publicly accessible place, they can be very shy. But are they that difficult to see? Your author has found that with a bit of effort, it is possible to increase your chances of seeing them.

The time available for overnight engineering work is very limited, so they have to arrive at the worksite almost immediately behind the last service train on that particular stretch of line. This means that they have to leave Ruislip depot before the end of traffic hours and can be seen from several stations prior to them closing for the night. When engineering trains leave Ruislip depot, if they are destined for anywhere on the Central Line, they will depart from the south end of the depot close to Ruislip Gardens station and run down the Central Line to their worksite. If they are bound for the short section of line between Ruislip and Uxbridge, they will leave via Ruislip siding and head west. Trains for all other destinations will leave via Ruislip siding, and pass through Ruislip, Ruislip Manor, Eastcote and Rayners Lane. Here they will either turn left onto the Metropolitan Line via Harrow-on-the-Hill, or they will turn right onto the Piccadilly Line towards South Harrow. Taking the Metropolitan, they can access the entire sub-surface network, the Jubilee and the Bakerloo. Taking the Piccadilly at Rayners Lane gives them access to the entire sub surface network, the Piccadilly, the Victoria and the Northern. In the morning, the trains have to come back, and they often leave the worksite just before the first service, so by the time they get close to Ruislip, the day's service has already commenced. If you are on any of the stations between Ruislip and Rayners Lane towards the end or the start of traffic hours, you stand a good chance of seeing engineering trains. Although they run as required and can run on any night, most overnight engineering trains leave Ruislip depot on Monday, Tuesday, Wednesday and Thursday evenings, returning to depot on Tuesday, Wednesday, Thursday and Friday mornings. When there is a large possession taking place over a weekend, there can be a procession of trains leaving Ruislip depot at the end of traffic on a Friday night. Trains returning from a weekend possession can often run in daylight hours. It is worth checking the Transport For London website for details of weekend engineering work for clues as to where trains may be found.

The above is a general guide and is in no way a guarantee that you will see some engineering trains, but it will certainly increase your chances.

The Engineering Fleet

Battery Locomotives

L15 (Metro-Cammell 1970)	L30 (Metro-Cammell 1965)*
L16 (Metro-Cammell 1970)	L31 (Metro-Cammell 1965)*
L17 (Metro-Cammell 1970)*	L32 (Metro-Cammell 1965)*
L18 (Metro-Cammell 1970)*	L44 (BREL Doncaster 1974)
L19 (Metro-Cammell 1970)	L45 (BREL Doncaster 1974)
L20 (Metro-Cammell 1964)	L46 (BREL Doncaster 1974)
L21 (Metro-Cammell 1964)	L47 (BREL Doncaster 1974)
L22 (Metro-Cammell 1965)*	L48 (BREL Doncaster 1974)
L23 (Metro-Cammell 1965)*	L49 (BREL Doncaster 1974)*
L24 (Metro-Cammell 1965)*	L50 (BREL Doncaster 1974)
L25 (Metro-Cammell 1965)*	L51 (BREL Doncaster 1974)*
L26 (Metro-Cammell 1965)	L52 (BREL Doncaster 1974)
L27 (Metro-Cammell 1965)*	L53 (BREL Doncaster 1974)
L28 (Metro-Cammell 1965)*	L54 (BREL Doncaster 1974)
L29 (Metro-Cammell 1965)	----------

*Refurbished with modified cab ends

Schöma Diesel Locomotives

L1 Britta Lotta	L6 Denise	L11 Joan
L2 Nikki*	L7 Annemarie	L12 Melanie
L3 Claire	L8 Emma*	L13 Michele
L4 Pam*	L9 Debora	L14 Carol
L5 Sophie*	L10 Clementine	----------

*Currently undergoing conversion to battery power

Track Maintenance Machines

TMM771	Plasser Theurer 1980	----------
TMM772	Plasser Theurer 1980	----------
TMM773	Plasser Theurer 1980	Named 'Alan Jenkins'
TMM774	Franz Plasser 2007	----------

Rail Wagons

RW495	RW802	RW806	RW810	RW814	RW818	RW822
RW505	RW803	RW807	RW811	RW815	RW819	RW823
RW506	RW804	RW808	RW812	RW816	RW820	RW824
RW801	RW805	RW809	RW813	RW817	RW821	RW825
						RW826

Spoil and Ballast Wagons (ex BR Turbot)

SB231	SB240	SB249	SB258	SB267	SB276	SB285
SB232	SB241	SB250	SB259	SB268	SB277	SB286
SB233	SB242	SB251	SB260	SB269	SB278	SB287
SB234	SB243	SB252	SB261	SB270	SB279	SB288
SB235	SB244	SB253	SB262	SB271	SB280	SB289
SB236	SB245	SB254	SB263	SB272	SB281	SB290
SB237	SB246	SB255	SB264	SB273	SB282	-----
SB238	SB247	SB256	SB265	SB274	SB283	-----
SB239	SB248	SB257	SB266	SB275	SB284	-----

Hopper Wagons

HW201	HW204	HW207	HW210	HW213	HW216	HW219
HW202	HW205	HW208	HW211	HW214	HW217	HW220
HW203	HW206	HW209	HW212	HW215	HW218	HW221
---	---	---	---	---	---	HW222

Cement Mixer Wagons

CM950	CM952	CM954
CM951	CM953	CM955

Deep Well Cable Drum Wagon

CW1053	CW1053	CW1053

General Purpose Wagons (ex JLE)

JLE1	JLE3	JLE5*	JLE7	JLE9	JLE11	JLE13
JLE2	JLE4	JLE6	JLE8	JLE10	JLE12	JLE14
---	---	---	---	---	---	JLE15

*Stored unserviceable

1962 Stock (*1959 stock)

DM(A)	T	NDM	DM(D)	DM(A)	T	NDM	NDM	DM(D)	Notes
1406	2406	9125*	1681	1682	---	9577	9459	1407	8-car Sandite 1
1570	---	9691	---	---	2440	---	9441	1441	5-car Sandite 2
1690	2682	---	1691	---	---	---	---	---	Acton Works (Spare)

General Purpose Wagons

GP901	GP909	GP917	GP925	GP933	GP941
GP902	GP910	GP918	GP926	GP934	---
GP903	GP911	GP919	GP927	GP935	---
GP904	GP912	GP920	GP928	GP936	---
GP905	GP913	GP921	GP929	GP937	---
GP906	GP914	GP922	GP930	GP938	---
GP907	GP915	GP923	GP931	GP939	---
GP908	GP916	GP924	GP932	GP940	---

High Deck Wagons

HD871	HD872	HD873	HD874	HD875	HD876

Match Wagons

MW956	MW957	MW958	MW959	MW960	MW961

A60/A62 Stock

DM(A)	T	T	DM(D)	Notes
5110	6110	6111	5111	-----------
5112	6112	6113	5113	Acton Works (spare)
5234	6234	6235	5235	-----------
---	6036	---	---	Rail Adhesion Car

1972 MkI Stock / 1967 Stock* Asset Inspection Train

DM(A)	T	DM(D)	DM(A)	T	DM(D)
3213	4213	3179*	3079*	4313	3313

Bogie Well Wagon (ex JLE)

JLE16	JLE17	JLE18
---	---	JLE19

Track Recording Train

L132	Ex 1960 Stock DM 3901
TRC666	Ex 1973 Stock trailer 514
L133	Ex 1960 Stock DM 3905

Cable Drum Wagon (ex JLE)

JLE20	JLE21	JLE22
---	---	JLE23

Diesel Hydraulic Crane (Twin Jib)

TRM627	TRM628

Diesel Hydraulic Crane

C623	C624	C6235	C6236

Running as train 710, the Metropolitan Line's A Stock Rail Adhesion Train led by 5110 passes through Harrow-on-the-Hill on its way to Amersham on 18 November 2014.

With L132 leading, the Track Recording Train is captured passing through Covent Garden on the Piccadilly Line while en route from Northfields depot to the Northern Line for overnight track recording. 4 December 2014.

Stored Stock

The below list shows withdrawn or stored stock and its last known location. The list does not include any stock that is stored away from LU metals.

1967 Stock

DM(A)	T	T	DM(D)	Notes
3060	4060	4160	3160	Acton Works
3061	4061	4161	3161	Acton Works
3067	4067	4167	3167	London Road (ambience training vehicles)
3075	4075	4175	3175	Acton Works
3022	---	---	3122	Acton Works
3007	---	---	3107	Acton Works

1972 MkI/MkII Stock

DM(A)	T	T	DM(D)	DM(D)	Notes
3202	4202	4302	3302	---	Acton Works (used for shunting)
---	4511	---	---	3411	Hainault depot (stored)
3229	4229	4329	3329	---	Aldwych

1983 Stock

DM(A)	T	DM(D)	Notes
3639	4639	3739	South Harrow (awaiting disposal)
3640	4640	3740	South Harrow (awaiting disposal)
3645	4645	3745	South Harrow (awaiting disposal)

A60/A62 Stock

T	Notes
6132	Acton Works (stored)

1973 Stock

T	DM(D)	Notes
566	366	Northfields

Despite being a system responsible for moving millions of people every day, the London Underground has the greatest respect for the history which brought it to where it is today. This is apparent in a lot of the stations, many of which have been sympathetically restored, and many of which are listed. The London Transport Museum in Covent Garden is well worth a visit and tells the story of not just the Underground, but also trams and buses in London. Not everything the LTM owns can be accommodated at Covent Garden, and they also have a large store at Acton where many trains, buses, trams and other artefacts are kept. The Acton Museum Store can be visited by appointment, but also stages a number of open days each year. Occasionally, heritage trains are run over parts of the network using old vehicles, and this has also included the use of steam.

London Transport Museum

Located in the corner of Covent Garden, the London Transport Museum displays several buses, a tram and a handful of rail vehicles, including Metropolitan-Vickers electric loco number 5 'John Hampden', Metropolitan Railway Beyer Peacock 'A' class 4-4-0T number 23, City & South London Railway electric loco number 13, 1938 Tube Stock car 11182 and Q23 car 4248. The museum has a fantastic gift shop which can be visited without having to pay to enter the museum. The closest Underground station is Covent Garden on the Piccadilly Line.

The museum is open all year round except Christmas Eve, Christmas Day and Boxing Day.

Opening times are:
Saturday to Thursday 10:00 to 18:00
Friday 11:00 to 18:00

At the time of compiling this book, entry costs were £16 for adults and £13.50 for concessions. Children under 17 enter for free, under 12s must be accompanied by an adult. These prices are subject to change, please check the London Transport Museum website before visiting: www.ltmuseum.co.uk

London Transport Museum Store, Acton

Unlike the main museum at Covent Garden, the Acton store is not open all year round. The public can only visit by appointment or there are a number of open days held each year. Details of open days, and how to arrange an appointment can be found on the London Transport Museum website (address above). It is well worth a visit and contains a wide variety of trains, stations signs, signalling equipment and even escalators. There is also a fine collection of trams and buses which include the prototype Routemaster bus RM1.

Heritage Train Trips

Occasionally heritage trains make it out onto the Underground network for a series of trips. These are often available to the public, but tickets usually need to be booked in advance through the LTM website. At the time of writing, no heritage train trips were being advertised, but there was talk of steam to Ealing Broadway and Watford during 2015. Vehicles that may be used on heritage trips are listed below:

1938 Tube Stock

Formed of 10012+012256+12048+11012, this 4 car set carries London Transport red livery and the internal advertising dates from 1988 when the unit was withdrawn from the Northern Line. At the time of writing, the unit was receiving attention in Acton Works.

Metropolitan-Vickers electric locomotive number 12 'Sarah Siddons'

Resplendent in Metropolitan Railway livery, this loco dates from 1923 and occasionally sees use on specials. It featured in the 150th Anniversary specials of 2013 and 2014.

1960 Tube Stock

Owned by Cravens Heritage Trains, this train was not passed for use on the Underground at the time of going to press, but it is the ambition of its owners for it to gain approval. In 2014, the unit moved under its own power on the Underground on test, and was also towed along the Central Line to take part in an event to mark 20 years since closure of the Ongar branch. More details can be found at www.eppingsignalcabin.com

Metropolitan Railway 'E' class 0-4-4T 'Metropolitan 1'

Known as 'Met 1', this steam loco dates from 1898. It normally lives at the Buckinghamshire Railway Centre and is hired in by the Underground when required. The loco saw use in 2013 and 2014 on the LU150 and Hammersmith & City 150 specials.

Ex GWR 'Prairie' tank L150

This is actually ex GWR loco 5521 which masquerades as a London Transport liveried L150. No locos of this type ever worked for London Transport or carried this livery, but the loco was painted this way to complement 'Met 1' on some of the 150th Anniversary workings. It is privately owned and hired in as required.

Ex BR 4TC set

The London Underground has an ex BR class 438 4TC set which carries a fake teak livery. The vehicles were BR numbers 70823, 71163, 76297 and 76324. They have been used on specials with 'Sarah Siddons' and various steam locomotives. They are normally based at Ruislip Depot.

The Cravens 1960 Tube Stock sits at Ongar station during an event to celebrate 20 years since closure of the Ongar branch. This photograph was taken during an evening photo shoot on 27 September 2014.

FURTHER INFORMATION

For those wishing to obtain more information about the London Underground, here are a few useful sources:

Mobile Apps

Smartphone apps exist that can aid trips on the London Underground either as an enthusiast, commuter or visitor. On Android, Tube Map by MXdata, and Tube Tracker are recommended, while on the iPhone, Tube Tracker and Tube Map Live are worth trying. There are new apps coming out all the time which can act as a 'sat nav' for users, guiding them round the system, or simply showing the next trains at a given location. There is even an app advising which stations have toilets! As many stations below ground now have wifi, these apps can be accessed and used on many Underground stations.

The Transport For London website (www.tfl.gov.uk)

The official website for all transport in London. This website gives details for service disruptions, forthcoming station closures and engineering works, ticketing details, maps and live departure boards. The information on this site also includes London Buses, Tramlink, River Boats etc.

London Transport Museum website (www.ltmuseum.co.uk)

This site can be used to plan your visit to the LTM, but also has an online shop which sells London Transport related gifts, books, DVDs etc. Details of forthcoming open days at Acton, heritage train trips and other events can be found here.

London Underground Railway Society (www.lurs.org.uk)

Membership to this society, dedicated to all things Underground, is highly recommended. For those who live close to London, friendly monthly meetings are held which include shows and talks. Speakers include enthusiasts, Underground employees, historians, people in LU making the 'big' decisions and even your author! The society produces a monthly magazine called 'Underground News', a quality publication with fleet news, historical articles, colour and black and white photographs, details of society events and news from around the Underground. The magazine is worth the membership fee alone. Details of how to join can be found at the web address above.

Epping & Ongar Railway (eorailway.co.uk)

For those wanting to visit the former Central Line Ongar branch, now a thriving preserved railway, this website will help you to plan your visit and details forthcoming events. The railway often operates steam trains, but also has a fleet of ex BR diesel locos. The railway is well worth a visit.

Transport For London Working Timetables
(www.tfl.gov.uk/corporate/publications-and-reports/working-timetables)

Up to date working timetables for each Underground line can be accessed through the TFL website using the link above. This gives all information regarding passenger workings, empty stock movements, train movements in and out of depots and even regularly used engineering train paths. These timetables are also excellent for identifying trains from their Train Number.

First and Last Tubes (www.tfl.gov.uk/modes/tube/first-and-last-tube)

Although this guide shows first and last trains for each line, this has been included in the book to illustrate when the Underground starts and finishes, and is in no way an in depth guide. It is worth visiting this webpage for a more detailed list of first and last trains, which can also be read in conjunction with the working timetables for a complete picture.

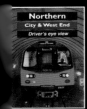